My Brother's Keeper

My Brother's Keeper

Life and Work of the Missionaries of the Poor

Carmen Vigo, Ph.D.

Monica Yoshida, Editor

Saint Benedict Press

Unless otherwise noted, Scripture quotations are from the Revised Standard Version—Second Catholic Edition (Ignatius Edition), copyright © 2006 National Council of the Churches of Christ in the United States of America. Used by permission. All rights reserved.

History of the Missionaries of the Poor and general information extracted from:

Missionaries of the Poor. Chronology and Events 2016. Milestones of the order from its foundation to April 26, 2016; *Candles in the Dark* by Joseph Pearce (Saint Benedict Press, 2012); and *Diary of a Ghetto Priest* by Father Richard Ho Lung (Missionaries of the Poor, 1998).

Cover design by Caroline K. Green

ISBN: 978-1-5051-0943-6

Published in the United States by
Saint Benedict Press
PO Box 410487
Charlotte, NC 28241
www.SaintBenedictPress.com

Wherever You Go

....

By Father Richard Ho Lung

Come with me and trust in me, leave all behind my friends.
Die to self, to selfishness, leave all behind my friends.
We will conquer flesh and conquer all the fires of hell.
We will show all men the way to God and we will conquer
death.

Wherever you go I will follow you, I'll live for you; I'll die for
you;
Wherever you go, I will follow you, I'll live for you, my Lord.
Whatever you ask, I will do for you. I'll work for you; I'll die
for you;
Whatever you say I will tell the world; I'll speak your truth,
my God.

Take my hands, lead me Lord, say the word, call my name,
Show the light, give commands, teach me Lord, You are the
way.

You must come with me, my friend,
You must leave the world behind, you must follow me.
You must walk the narrow road,
Leave the broad and common road, come follow me.

Whenever you call we will rise and walk, and go the road,
and walk the way;
Whenever you call we will answer you,
We'll hear your Word, Oh Lord. Obey your word, my God.

CONTENTS

CONTENTS

FOREWORD

By Joseph Pearce

THERE are relatively few occasions in anyone's life that can truly be called life changing. It is rare indeed that something happens to us which is so startling, so seismic in its impact, that we are never the same again. One such moment happened to me when I first visited the Missionaries of the Poor in their home among the homeless in the middle of the ghetto in Kingston, Jamaica. In truth, it must be confessed, I was a reluctant visitor, a resentful pilgrim to this shrine to the suffering Christ. I had been asked to write a biography of Father Richard Ho Lung, the MOP's charismatic founder and had only accepted after praying that this burden might pass from me. Having had my prayers answered in a way that contradicted my desires, I embraced the task of writing the book as an act of Lenten penance, taking it up as a cross that I was not too willing to carry. It was thus that I first visited the brothers in Jamaica. I did not know what I was letting myself in for, and, having arrived, I did not know what had hit me.

I recall my first visit to Bethlehem, the brothers' home for seriously sick and disabled children. The stench of urine, faeces, and sweat hit me as I crossed the threshold, stopping me in my tracks as surely as if I'd hit a brick wall. In front of me was a menagerie of deformed humanity. I was repelled—and guilty as hell at my own repulsion and the heart of stone from which it sprang. It was then that I saw the face of Christ. I saw it in the face of a paralysed young girl, supine in a cot. She caught my eye and her face beamed into the broadest grin I'd ever seen. Transfixed by this transfiguration, I walked forward and picked her up. I then carried her with me as I walked from cot to cot, from bed to bed, from the bedridden to the bedridden, babies, toddlers and older children, all being cared for by the white-robed brothers. It had changed my life. I had plunged into depths that I didn't know existed and had emerged, as if baptized, from the shallows of myself into something deeper.

Having had this experience, I understood Father Ho Lung when he told me that he welcomed visitors from the affluent world, from the world of excess, not because he and the brothers needed their help but because the visitors needed to experience joyful suffering with Christ on his cross, which is the very spirit and the motto of the Missionaries of the Poor. Those who have this experience are forever changed for the better. What a gift!

Needless to say, I embarked upon the writing of my book with a newfound enthusiasm, lifting the cross and finding that the burden was light indeed. And light in both senses of the word, which is why I called my book *Candles in the Dark*.

This new book offers a snapshot of the work of the brothers in their own words, the fruit of the interviews that Mrs. Vigo has conducted during her own visits to Jamaica. Those who read the following pages are not likely to have a life-changing experience—we need to get our hands dirty and our hearts clean by visiting the brothers in their native home for that to happen—but they will get a priceless glimpse of the Missionaries of the Poor who are changing lives with the joy of their own suffering which has its life-giving source in the suffering of the crucified Lord.

WHERE IS YOUR BROTHER?

*Then the LORD said to Cain, "Where is Abel
your brother?" He answered, "I do not know; am
I my brother's keeper?"*

Gn 4:9

IN today's world, we are tempted by material attractions—money, power, honor, and sensual pleasure—and many of us are seduced into focusing our lives on getting our share. Modern society assesses our worth by our possessions, not by our righteousness. In the process of keeping up with these worldly pressures, many of us become prone to being dominated by these powers, which become our masters, causing us to no longer recognize the voice of God.

Having fallen prey to these worldly values, narcissism and greed have seeped into our communities. In the process, not only have we foregone the ways to fulfill our deepest longing for happiness, but we have also eliminated God as the center of our lives and forgotten the poor and the needy. Pope Francis has said, "Almost without being aware of it, we end up being incapable of feeling compassionate for the outcry of the poor, weeping for other people's pain, and feeling for them as if this was the responsibility of somebody else and not our own." The world convinces us that worldly power and material possessions will fulfill our deep yearnings. But things cannot fulfill our deepest longing for love.

The quest for happiness has been a topic of inquiry throughout history. St. Augustine cried out after exhausting all worldly ways to find happiness, "Lord, you made us for yourself and our hearts are restless until they rest in you." Blessed Cardinal John Henry Newman (d. 1890) wrote:

> I am speaking of men . . . before they have given
> their hearts to the world, which promises them
> true good, then cheats them, and then makes
> them believe there is no truth anywhere, and
> that they were fools for thinking it. But before
> that time they have desires after things above
> this world, which then embody some form of
> this world, because they have no other way at
> all of realizing them. If they are in humble life,
> they dream of becoming their own masters,
> rising in the world, and securing an indepen-
> dence; if in a higher rank, they have ambitious
> thoughts of gaining a name and exercising
> power. While their hearts are thus unsettled,
> Christ comes to them, if they will receive him,
> and promises to satisfy their great need, this
> hunger and thirst which wearied them. He does
> not wait till they have learned to ridicule high
> feelings as mere romantic dreams: he comes to
> the young, he has them baptized betimes, and

then promises them, and in a higher way, those
unknown blessings which they yearn after.

In answer to the heart's deepest longing, Jesus told the
rich young man, "If you would be perfect, go, sell what you
possess and give to the poor, and you will have treasure in
heaven; and come, follow me" (Mt 19:21).

The call to heed the message of the gospel is a challenging one to answer in our world. But it is not impossible.
The young men and women of the Missionaries of the
Poor have responded to that inner call for happiness by
looking to the poorest of the poor. Rejecting the world's
enticements that lead to emptiness, they have received and
embraced God's love and committed their lives to sharing
it with others.

These missionaries give themselves away to serve the
least of our brothers. They choose to bind themselves to the
poor and become one with them. They are like stars shining in the darkness, a group of brave young men who rose
from the ashes in the slums of Jamaica and other parts of
the world to follow Jesus in the radical way of total poverty.

Emptying themselves of all possessions and attachments,
they live in utter simplicity. As they put their lives at the
total service of the Mystical Body of Christ in the poor, they
keep their eyes fixed on Jesus on the cross. And their lives
are dedicated not simply to sharing in his most agonizing
moments. But rather, they share his joy in his last breath,
death, and resurrection. Nailed to the cross, they reach up a
hand to give him a drink. They know he is thirsty.

By example, they have proven that by dying to themselves and accepting the cross and suffering, they have

discovered the secret of living life to the fullest. With their work, they have responded to the call of God: "Where is your brother?" Our brother is every one of the poorest of the poor, the sick, the dying, and the discards of society.

The Missionaries of the Poor serve our brothers day and night, embracing them and helping them to bear their own crosses. These holy missionary brothers and sisters are the contemporary faces of Simon of Cyrene, helping Jesus to carry his cross in his suffering mystical Body.

As a frequent visitor to the Missionaries of the Poor in Jamaica, I have experienced firsthand the happiness of these brothers and sisters. A unique sense of peace and fulfillment pervades their lives and the lives of all the residents and visitors that come in contact with them.

There is a blessed joy with the Missionaries of the Poor that is not woven from the fabric of a materialistic world, a joy that can only radiate from the very presence of God in their midst and among the people to whom they minister. There, among God's poor, is found a holy delight which can only come from responding to God's call: "Our brothers are here with us, under our care."

Chapter One

FEET OF CLAY

Missionaries of the Poor:
The Call, the Vows, and the Life

*We, Brothers, love them! They had no home,
slept out in the streets under the stars, lonely,
forgotten hungry, half naked, caked with mud,
dressed in old faded rags. They have no father,
no mother, no sister, no brother, no job, nothing
and no one. We can't imagine what it must feel
like! Totally rejected, no loved one, often cursed
and reviled and rejected by everyone. We love
them. We take them to ourselves. They have such
a great capacity to love, to be grateful.*

—Brother (Father) Hayden Augustine,

MOP

WHEN Father Richard Ho Lung was still a Jesuit priest, in July 1981, he set out to spend a month with a group of young students in the hills of Newcastle, Jamaica, leading them in a retreat of intense prayer and discernment. The result of this retreat was the decision to found the Brothers of the Poor that same year. In 1983, Father Richard Ho Lung fully resolved to leave his Jesuit community to pursue a new path of radical poverty. From

1

the time of the founding of the Brothers of the Poor, Father Ho Lung has been, in his own words, "haunted by the presence of God." He formally petitioned for an indult of secularization, Praevio Experimento, which was granted on December 5, 1983, by the Sacred Congregation for Religious. In 1989, Father Ho Lung was formally incardinated as a diocesan priest of the Archdiocese of Kingston.

The newly formed Brothers of the Poor had an inauspicious beginning. Only six of those who joined the retreat in the hills took the initial vows on July 19, 1981. Later, three of the initial group drifted away, leaving only Father Ho Lung and two students, Hayden Augustine, from Trinidad, and Brian Kerr, from Jamaica. The community grew slowly and steadily and would not adopt the name "Missionaries of the Poor" (MOP) until 1992.

These homeless beggars found temporary accommodation at the home of a friend where they shared one room, which they filled with so many books that they had to sleep on the roof. Eventually, the Jesuit Archbishop of Kingston, Samuel Carter, gave them the use of a former Jesuit house on Monroe Road. Later, in 1990, a benefactor purchased a former Chinese school for them, which they named Corpus Christi; this became the brothers' first permanent home and motherhouse.

The early work of the Brothers of the Poor revolved around ministry to the residents of Eventide, a crowded and squalid government-run health institution. There, all the residents were neglected, and young handicapped girls were often abducted from the wards and raped. The beds and floors of the wards were covered in excrement and urine. The residents were starving to death. Some of them were eaten by rats while still alive. Father Ho Lung and his friends would regularly visit these residents, binding their wounds, shaving, bathing, and feeding the most distressed. Troubled by the appalling conditions of the ward and the indifference of the politicians and bureaucrats, Father Richard Ho Lung published a booklet exposing the hideous conditions at Eventide, thus making the outside world aware of the disgraceful circumstances of the center and shaming the Jamaican government for so poorly running this institution. This information touched many people, bringing in money and help. It also raised harsh criticisms by the government, which insisted that he should withdraw the publication. Father Ho Lung refused to hide the truth and never wavered in his firm support for the residents despite intense criticism and death threats.

As donations poured in, the Brothers of the Poor continued helping the homeless, the destitute, and unjustly incarcerated men. Donations made to the Brothers of the Poor made it possible for Father Richard Ho Lung to open the first apostolate centers in 1984. The brothers, totally depending on charity donations, freely ran these centers. This was followed by opening the first overseas missions in Warangal in Andhra Pradesh, Southern India, in 1992, and in the same year by the second one in Naga City in the Philippines. From these groundbreaking beginnings, the MOP continued expanding, opening later missions in Haiti, Uganda, Kenya, Indonesia, and the United States.

The motto of the MOP is "Joyful Service with Christ on the Cross." The MOP know that by serving the poor they

serve God. "As you did it to the least of these my brethren,
you did it to me" (Mt 25:40). This was the drive and inspiration of their founder, Father Richard Ho Lung:

> I wanted others to also experience the joy of
> giving without expecting anything. This is
> what inspired me to begin the Missionaries
> of the Poor where men will dedicate them-
> selves wholly and completely in free service
> of His broken Body in the poor. If the door
> of our eternal Beatitude was flung open for us
> because of Jesus' brokenness on the cross, then
> how can we charge Jesus in the poor? Freely,
> He gave of Himself for us in order that we may
> have life abundant, then how can we not freely
> serve Him in the lives of the poor? We cannot
> hold back anything from Him. Our own lives
> are a gift from Him; therefore, to give Him our
> whole life is nothing but a return of what he has
> given to us. Giving brings great joy! The Lord
> reminds us that the more we give, the more we
> receive.

Each member of the MOP owns nothing and possesses
nothing. Everything they have belongs to the community.
Whatever is given to them is given to the community.
Whatever belongs to the community belongs to the poor
whom they serve. They do not charge anyone for the ser-
vices they offer. All is done free of cost. "You have received
without pay, give without pay" (Mt 10:8).

To be the founder of this community, says Father
Richard Ho Lung, is very simple. "Do whatever he says," as

Mary tells the servants at the wedding feast of Cana. Hence, a religious community of brothers sprung forth to glorify the Lord and to do his will. Though they are on a small island which is only 2 percent Catholic, the MOP have brought forth a community of joyful, self-sacrificing men; they have made a joyful noise celebrating God's incredibly rich life by living out the word of God.

The brothers come from many corners of the world: Jamaica, Trinidad, India, the Philippines, Uganda, Kenya, Vietnam, Guatemala, Belize, and Indonesia, and from all kinds of backgrounds and levels of formation. They all gave their "Fiat" and their lives to God and joined a community to live by the commandment: "You shall love the Lord your God with all your heart, and with all your soul, and with all your mind. . . . You shall love your neighbors as yourself" (Mt 22:37, 39). Many of the brothers come from very humble families; some join the order straight from high school, others after completing college education. They heard the call of God and followed it. They are chosen from among the poor and the rich, regardless of the levels of education, for God sees all as his creations.

Once the candidates join the MOP institute, they go through nine years of formation, which comprises six months to one year "aspirancy." During this period they are introduced to the life and work of the MOP. This is a time of discernment that takes place in one's own country. The formation continues for another six months of "postulancy," in which they are given time to consider if religious life is God's will for them. If they persevere, then they go to the Institute headquarters in Jamaica to continue their formation during a two-year novitiate. The first canonical year emphasizes prayer and contemplation, and includes a forty-day retreat. The second apostolic year emphasizes the work of the apostolate of the MOP in their various centers in the slums of the city. This is followed by the "Juniorate," when the brothers take their temporary vows at the end of the sixth year, and keep on growing in formation and knowledge of the mission and works of the Institute. "Seniorate" is the final step when the individual is admitted to the order, and the perpetual profession of the vows are made for a lifetime's service.

The overall formation of the brothers is deeply rooted in the Jesuit tradition and in the rules of the life and work of Mother Teresa of Calcutta and her Sisters of Charity. During the formation period, the MOP are taught Scripture, Church history, Church documents, literature, nursing, music, ethics, rules, and spirituality of the Order.

The members of the MOP take vows of poverty, celibacy, obedience, and a fourth vow: to give free service to the poor. The additional fourth vow was intended to ensure that the MOP would always stay unequivocally focused on the needs of the poorest and most needy members of society. No brother can have a personal bank account, keep money with him, nor can any brother start a business intended for profit. Trusting fully in Divine Providence, the MOP rely on the generosity of fellow Christians to provide for their needs. Their whole life is centered on prayer and service.

This following is a description of the daily life of the MOP provided by Brother (Father) Hayden Augustine:

Full of love and full of human foibles. We have feet of clay but long to be holy and unite ourselves with the Lord, our wonderful Lord.

When we rise in the morning, we are in silence, trying to recollect as best as we can the presence of the Lord, our amazing God whom we serve morning, noon and night. We sometimes struggle to remember him, but we never stop reaching out of our flesh, out of our human weaknesses, to see him and be united with him.

Rising at 5:30 a.m., we are in silence. By 5:45 a.m., we are in the chapel. We chant the Divine Office. We listen to the Word of God and the preaching. We give ourselves to the Lord in the Sacrifice of the Mass. We consume the Body and Blood of Christ.

At 6:45 a.m., we have Exposition of the Blessed Sacrament. What a wonder it is to have Christ with us exposed—his Real Presence to us! Yes, this is the God who performed such great miracles, who fed five thousand with only five loaves and two fish, who stilled the storm at sea, and conquered the devil. Then he died for us on the cross, crucified, rejected, and reviled. Now, here he is in the Blessed Sacrament, presenting himself to us again. He just wants to be with us, so great is his love for us.

After Mass, we have breakfast in silence. We reflect on union with the Lord, the Word of God, and the miracle of his Presence to us, sinful men.

Then down to the centers. Our brothers are assigned a home to work all day: Faith Center, Jacob's Well, Good Shepherd, The Lord's Place, and Bethlehem Home.

Six hundred and fifty homeless and destitute residents live with us. Our work never ends at the centers: cooking, feeding, cleaning, and washing dishes. Then there are the medicines, followed by sweeping away the debris and changing the residents' clothes. If the beds are filled with mess or wet with urine, we get at it. We brush their teeth, shave the men, and then shower everyone.

In the midst of this, the early morning sun warms our hearts. The residents—so many of them—can't walk and are physically or mentally challenged.

We brothers love them! They had no home, slept out in the streets under the stars, lonely, forgotten hungry, half-naked, caked with mud, dressed in old faded rags. They have no father, no mother, no sister, no brother, no job, nothing and no one. We can't imagine what it must feel like! Totally rejected, no loved one, often cursed and reviled and rejected by everyone. We love them. We take them to ourselves. They have such a great capacity to love, to be grateful—always giving thanks for the home we provide for them.

Near midday we sing spiritual songs with our homeless residents. It's full of gladness with tambourines and maracas in praise of the Lord.

After that, the brothers give a lunch of rice and beans, maybe dumplings and callaloo, and on a special day, a little chicken.

In the afternoon, our residents help to feed each other, clean up, and take care of each other. They chatter a lot, then they get a little drowsy, especially the elderly. Some sleep in the wheelchairs, others go to their beds. Others sweep the floors, dispose of the garbage or help the brother with house duties.

There are some who go to the hospitals. Sometimes we have Mass during the afternoon, and that is a real treat. There is gardening, washing of clothes, and preparation of goods in the storeroom.

What is our life like? It is a joyful carrying of the cross of Christ. That is our life; it never ends. The poor are our lives. The brothers are always there. We are brothers, really brothers, present to the most needy—day in, and day out, loving them, protecting them, praying with them, until death do us part.

After a day's work or evening shift, we go back to our monasteries. There is recitation of the Psalms, spiritual reading, and the rosary for one and a half hours.

At 7:15 p.m., there is supper, followed by house duties and community recreation. At 9:00 p.m., we bring closure to the day with the reading of Psalms and silence before our beloved Lord and God. We close our sleepy

eyes full of gratefulness and thanksgiving, cra-
dled in the arms of our loving Lord.

The brothers live and work in the slums, leading a life
rooted in charity and joyful giving to the homeless, sick,
and destitute. The MOP offer them shelters equipped with
electricity and clean running water, provide them meals,
beds, medicines, clothes, and spiritual counseling. The
army of young and dedicated brothers exudes joy and
peace wherever they go. Their lives reflect the joy and inner
peace that only comes from living in the presence of God.

The overarching priority of the MOP is evident in their
motto, "Servitium Dulce cum Christo Crucifixo" (Joyful
Service with Christ on the Cross), which was unveiled
when they were granted papal recognition as a Religious
Institute of Diocesan Rite in 1997. The MOP serve tens of
thousands of the most needy human beings, some afflicted
with leprosy and HIV, others with deep mental or physical
handicaps, who could not survive on their own in the slums
of the cities. These discarded members of the society are
brought to the centers and remain there under the care of
the MOP until they die.

As a visitor to their monasteries and apostolate centers
in Kingston, I had the privilege to share in the life, prayers,
and work of the brothers. I was awed by their relentless
service and love for the residents, seven days a week, from
early morning to the deep evening. It became fully clear
to me that they can only do it by the love of God that sus-
tains them in their demanding and challenging vocation.
They have indeed been called, seduced, and pierced by
God's love. As Charles Montalembert in the nineteenth

century asked, "But who is then this invisible Lover who died upon a gibbet nineteen centuries ago, and who thus draws to himself youth, beauty, and love? Who appears to souls with a splendor and fascination which they cannot resist?" Father Richard Ho Lung clearly articulated a response: "The brothers have found in the depths of their heart, where God abides, the love that they might not even know or ever believe was there before." The MOP have been called and seduced by God and have surrendered to his call with their personal "Fiat." As St. Irenaeus of Lyons said, "The glory of God is man fully alive," and truly, the MOP are fully alive. One can really see the glory of God shining through their prayers and works.

Anyone visiting the MOP centers can see and appreciate the joy and happiness of the residents, those beautiful human beings whose worth and dignity are often not recognized by the standards established by the world. Only those who cannot see the divine in the least of these brothers can deny their dignity and right to life. After all, is not having the opportunity to wipe and dry the face of the suffering Jesus on the cross the greatest privilege that any human being can have? Yet, to some extent, we all have these opportunities in our midst. The MOP, with their lives and example, open our hearts and minds and challenge us to go into the depths of our hearts to discover the call and the love of God to serve the least of our brothers.

The MOP are not merely social workers; they are truly servants for the broken Body of Christ. Their work is a labor of love. They lay down their lives every day for the lives of the least of our brothers and sisters. The MOP have chosen to nurture a culture of life. They choose life and share in the misery of others as the only way to happiness, they kneel in a state of nothingness and rise with the resurrected Christ. They chose "Mary, Cause of Our Joy" as their patron, and Mary leads them to die with the crucified Jesus, and to rise with him.

The lives of the MOP can be summarized in the words of its founder, Father Ho Lung: "To be at oneness with the poor, the suffering, the blind, the deaf, the widows, the orphans. To be pure of any selfish desire, then to die at the foot of the Cross and to kneel in a state of nothingness before the Almighty . . . that is what brings happiness."

> Can it be a dream, that in the end man will find his joy only in deeds of light and mercy, and not in cruel pleasures as now? . . . I firmly believe that it is not and at the time is at hand. People laugh and ask: "When will that time come and does it look like coming?" I believe that with Christ's help we shall accomplish this great thing. . . . So it will be with us, and our people will shine forth in the world, and all men will say: "The stone which the builders rejected has become the cornerstone of the building."
>
> —Fyodor Dostoevsky, *Brothers Karamazov*

Chapter Two

FATHER, IT IS EASTER!

Father Hayden Augustine, MOP

The LORD is my Shepherd, I shall not want;
he makes me lie down in green pastures.
He leads me beside still waters;
he restores my soul.
He leads me in paths of righteousness
for his name's sake.
Even though I walk through the valley of the
shadow of death,
I fear no evil;
for you are with me;
your rod and your staff,
they comfort me.

Ps 23:1-4

HAYDEN Augustine went from his native Trinidad to Jamaica to join the novitiate of the Jesuits. His plan was to become a Jesuit like Father Richard Ho Lung, whom he met while receiving spiritual direction and guidance from the Society.

He was one of the twenty-six young men who, on July 19, 1981, went on a thirty-day retreat with Father Richard Ho Lung in the mountains in Jamaica, where they remained in intense prayer and discernment. At the end of the retreat, Father Ho Lung invited them to do missionary work with him permanently. Hayden and five others from the group accepted the invitation to dedicate their lives to serve the poor and needy. This group laid the foundation for the order that would come to be the MOP. Thus, Father Hayden Augustine became one of the early founding members of the Missionaries.

He describes this early experience in his own words, "After the 1981 retreat with Father Ho Lung, I went back home to pack up the bags and came back to join the newly formed group of the Brothers of the Poor, which was a pious union. For two months we lived in a friend's house, and by November we moved to the former Jesuit house where Father Ho Lung had lived for nine years, which was vacated and donated to him by Archbishop Carter of Kingston. A few years later, we moved to a former Chinese school. We named it Corpus Christi, which since then became our motherhouse."

Father Hayden's parents were very devout and prayerful Catholics. He has two sisters and four brothers. They all attended a Catholic school run by the Holy Ghost Fathers, which provided them with a solid religious foundation. Inspired by the Holy Ghost Fathers, Hayden wanted to devote his life to the service of humanity. Three out of the five boys became priests—one of them joining the Holy Ghost Fathers—and the two older brothers got married. He remembers his father as very strict and his mother as a very devout, loving, and gentle person. He thinks he learned devoutness from his mother and the stability and firmness from his father.

Which quality of Father Ho Lung attracted you the most to decide to follow in his footsteps?

I was twenty-one years old when I joined Father Ho Lung in his mission to serve the poor. Father Ho Lung's profound spirituality and words in action drew me to join him in his mission. Father Ho Lung was very impressive and inspiring with a very intense and profound spirituality. We discussed many issues of life that deeply affected and drew me to follow in his footsteps. When I met Father Ho Lung, he still was a Jesuit priest but always wanted to be among the poor, visiting the sick at Eventide and going to the slums to work among the poor.

Father Hayden, can you describe some of your early experiences that deeply moved you?

This one day in 1980, I was following Father Ho Lung around the slums and walked onto this piece of land. It was pure dirt with no grass, and there were hundreds of people gathering and screaming. They were very agitated, expressing intense fear for what was going to happen that night. They were afraid to be shot. This was the pre-election year, a very intense period of instability and corruption in Jamaica. People were forced to vote for some of the individuals running for election. The people gathered there were afraid to be killed. To reassure them, Father Ho Lung took all the women and children out of that gathering area in the slum to the Jesuit community where he was living with five other Jesuits. This crowd of people stayed there for five days; they camped, cooked, and slept outside

the Jesuit residence. It was something that the Jesuits were
not too thrilled about. Father Ho Lung had that special charisma to appease the crowds totally; I had never seen this in
my life. This particular experience struck me deeply. I saw
with my own eyes that the Lord hears the cries of the poor;
the poor were crying for protection, for deliverance from
dangers, and Father Ho Lung answered them.

How did you spend your first years as Brothers of the Poor?

We had no apostolate centers yet, so we visited Eventide
Home, a squalid government-run institution for the mentally sick and destitute, three days per week. I also started
to study in the seminary to become a priest. Brian Kerr,
another of the founding members, started to study for the
priesthood two years later. We were only six brothers, two
from United States. One member of the initial group left to
start the Mustard Seed and another one from the United
States also left. For the first five months we were only four,
and we grew gradually and steadily. Our group was small
but true. We were focused and authentic, and that was what
mattered to us. We didn't wear habits; I was wearing shorts
until Father Ho Lung asked me to wear long trousers. We
were not a congregation but simply a pious union, which is
a small group of people that takes a pledge to live together
under the permission of the Church. Father Ho Lung was
still technically a Jesuit then; he hadn't left the Jesuit order
yet, and it is fair to say that if things did not work out, he
would have gone back to the Jesuits. He was doing in our

group what he was doing with the Jesuits already, working for the poor but at a deeper level. Earlier, as a Jesuit, he had also started a music group, "Father Ho Lung and Friends," composing songs and musical shows. When Father Ho Lung was part of the Jesuit order, he was also lecturing in the university and doing part time work with the poor. He now had a much stronger call to work full time with the poor. We were the men to make it happen.

From the beginning of the Brothers of the Poor, Father Ho Lung wanted us to have a structure. Keeping a daily schedule was important, he taught us that ringing the bell for the various activities was a reminder of the voice of God calling us; it structured the day and called us to work or to prayer. We had daily mass, prayers, and chants. We could not have envisioned the order as we see it today, but we were open and trusted that wherever the Lord would lead us, we would follow. We had a profound commitment and we were true to our mission. And God rewarded us.

Did Father Ho Lung want you all to become priests?

I was ordained a priest in 1987 and Brian Kerr in 1991. Father Ho Lung from the beginning was not sure that we should be priests or brothers; he didn't want us to be concerned only about saying Mass. His concern was that we were not just good priests but also followers of Christ. He wanted us to minister to the needy with the love of Christ, so "Brothers of the Poor" was an appropriate name for our community. The priesthood then was the preferred ministry for the men, but from very early it became clear that priesthood would not be the lifestyle of the men in our order. We wanted to live like brothers. We are a brotherhood. In 1997, we got the official legal canonical status as Religious Institute of Diocesan Rite and celebrated it on the feast of the Annunciation in March 1998, when we made it official. We finally had approval from the Church with canonical status. From the late eighties, we were planning to expand out of Jamaica. In 1992, we went to India and started getting many new vocations.

How did the order evolve?

In our institute, we took one day at the time, step by step, and it evolved gradually and steadily. As I teach the young brothers, this life is not for the feeble but for those who can endure. There were pressure points in our life, but nothing that the Lord did not give us the grace to endure.

I went first to India and later to Kampala, Uganda, to recruit new vocations and establish new apostolate centers. The Holy Spirit and Divine Providence were leading us. Divine Providence determined our decision how to start a new mission: the location and the construction. It takes a lot of trust; there is no financial gain or security. It is for spreading the kingdom of God; there are no economic or personal benefits involved. All that we do is to serve God and the people. We opened new missions in India, the Philippines, and Africa, Uganda in 2000, followed by Kenya in 2007.

How did you overcome the difficulties in the order?

The Lord God is almighty and gives strength to the faint. Prayer is the bedrock of our lives; only after prayer can we work. It can't be the other way around. In prayer and contemplation we encounter the real flesh of Christ, this is the lesson I learned from Father Ho Lung. Life never came to the point that we thought that this was impossible. In early years there were attacks to our community, to our work, and to our ideas. Father Ho Lung would deal with these issues; he would deal with the government, with the media, and with any and all institutions. Father Ho Lung was the bedrock in Christ. He was not disturbed by any of the attacks; he never doubted that he had done the right thing. He stood up for the truth.

I gave them your word, and the world has hated them because they are not of the world, even as I am not of the world. (Jn 17:14)

Describe some special moments in your life that left a deep impression of the presence of God in your work.

In 2009, when I was in Uganda, we had big Masses every Sunday, one for adults and another one for the children. On Easter Sunday, 2009, the morning was really dark, cold, and gloomy, with a sprinkling of rain. That morning, I was thinking that nobody was going to come to Mass. Thirty minutes before the Mass was to start, something extraordinary happened: over two thousand children showed up.

I was dumbfounded! I thought, this is impossible! I asked
the children, "Why did you come?"

"Father, it is Easter!" they all shouted.

During Mass, when it was time to sing Gloria, and with
the bells ringing, the brightest sun broke out through the
clouds. At the Gloria! They were mostly poor children,
walking for miles to attend church, not deterred by the
weather or the long walk to get to church. It was Easter
Sunday and there was light! It was like at the singing of the
Gloria, God opened the heavens and let the sun shine to
remind us that he was there.

Another special moment happened when I was in India
in 1996. After four years of living there, my visa was not
renewed, and I was being expelled; I was literally being
kicked out. I had gone three weeks above the expiration
date of my visa before I got my ticket to fly back to Jamaica.
My papers, therefore, were not quite in order. I was anxious
because I was taking two other brothers to Jamaica with
me, but they were leaving on a later flight. They had not
travelled on their own before and I wanted to see them go
through. While I was at Bombay Airport waiting for my
flight, I saw an off-duty immigration officer. I went to him
and explained that I was traveling to Jamaica with two
brothers who were leaving after me and I wanted to make
sure that they would go through without problems. The off-
duty officer was a kind man and told me not to worry, that
he would make sure the brothers would leave as arranged.

In the meantime, I was trying to go through passport
control when it was the last call to board my plane. The
flight attendant was calling me by the loudspeakers to

board immediately. As soon as I went to passport control, the immigration officer yelled at me, "This is not right!" "Wait there!" I knew it was the last call to check in to board the plane and I was worried. All of a sudden, I saw the immigration officer that I had talked to—I found out later that he was the head of immigration. I pointed out to him that I was being called to board immediately, so he signaled the agent to let me go through. This was definitely from God! The immigration head didn't know my situation with my visa. He assumed all was fine and he told the passport control agent to let me go. There is no rational explanation how God in his provident care was helping me. I thought, "Who am I to get all these favors?" The Lord walks ahead of you, anticipates your needs, and never disappoints you.

As you move forward, what do you see ahead? Do you have a vision?

I focus in the present. At this time, my focus is teaching, giving retreats, and providing spiritual direction for the newly arriving brothers. I am satisfied with this work. I am getting older and more conservative; I can't jump on trains and buses anymore, like I used to do when I was young. I let the younger brothers travel and jump trains and buses as I did. There are great expectations for new expansions of our missionary work, but for the time being, a few sites are on the horizon in the western world. Father Ho Lung is looking at Atlanta and Trinidad. Expansion requires local vocations; we need an increase in vocations in general in the Institute. Right now, some of the novices leave, while new ones arrive. I need to give these young men a sense of stability, security, and the certainty that they are in the right place, because sometimes they feel insecure. The world is too alluring—all those gadgets and material things. They need to give up everything. It is a major demand on their lives. During my upbringing, my daddy was always at home. This gave me a very strong sense of belonging. The brothers look up to us, and we have to give them stability as I had when I was growing up. They want a brother and a father figure in their lives. I need to be an example to them; I need to lead them to Jesus.

> *My sheep hear my voice, and I know them,*
> *and they follow me; and I give them eternal life,*
> *and they shall never perish, and no one shall*
> *snatch them out of my hand.* (Jn 10:27)

How do you embrace the poor?

This is almost second nature. I worked in the Faith Center for eight years. They are people, they are broken people; but we are not therapists. We are brothers to them. We love them and see Jesus in their brokenness. We must pray and persevere in prayer to persevere in our commitment to serve the poor. Some of our brothers do not persevere, and leave; we believe it is for lack of commitment to our mission, not so much for our vows of poverty or style of life. Other priests and religious people in opulent orders and opulent diocese still leave [their vocations] too. It is not because they take care of the poor like we do; it is because of a lack of commitment, lack of prayer, lack of vision, lack of spirituality. They have all the comforts of the world and still leave. It is a deeper problem; it is lack of prayer and commitment, they need to focus on serving the Lord, on following Christ. Father Ho Lung wants us to be simple servants, to focus on serving Christ on the cross and serving the crucified Christ in the poor with joy. This is our charisma; this is what is going to save Christianity.

How can we change the world?

There is a hunger in the world. Pope Francis is so attractive because of his message: his call is to serve the poor. The world has gone mad. How can we put it together? Why do successful people who have everything—two or three marriages, women, health, money, and fame—still end their lives by committing suicide? We need to keep the vision to save those who are lost. The things of the world do not satisfy the hunger of the soul. In the world, there is a hunger that only God can satiate and people look to satiate it with the wrong things. Here, we live a very positive life; we have positive moments like the concerts and when the brothers pour themselves out to serve the poor. We have a vision of expanding. Father Ho Lung has a vision—the renewal of the Church and renewal of the faith. The order is growing. The MOP Sisters order was installed five years ago. Our mission is to move forward and to renew the face of the earth.

Can you tell us something about you that you want us to know?

I have had an incredibly happy life! I used to be a very timid person due to my upbringing, timid and very closed. In Jamaica, Father Ho Lung brought me out of myself and I am very grateful and happy here. I am very grateful to be introduced to the spiritual world. I am happy to be in the kingdom of God. I have joy beyond what words can describe.

> I give you thanks, O LORD, with my whole
>   heart;
>   before the angels I sing your praise;
>   I bow down toward your holy temple
>   and give thanks to your name for your mercy
>   and your faithfulness;
>   for you have exalted above everything
>   your name and your word.
>   On the day I called, you answered me,
>   my strength of soul you increased. (Ps
>   138:1-3)

Chapter Three

JOYFUL SURRENDER

Most Reverend Father Richard Ho Lung, MOP

My beloved speaks and says to me:
"Arise, my love, my dove, my fair one,
    and come away;
for behold, the winter is past,
    the rain is over and gone.
The flowers appear on the earth,
    the time of pruning has come,
and the voice of the turtledove
    is heard in our land.

                                             Sg 2:10-12

THE Most Reverend Superior General and Founder of the Missionaries of the Poor, Father Richard Ho Lung, after thirty-three years serving as Superior General since he founded the order, relinquished his duties on March 25, 2014 to his younger brothers. Most Reverend Anil Minj is presently the Superior General of the Institute.

Father Ho Lung, how do you feel on passing the leadership as Superior General?

I have to build up a new set of young people to give them the opportunity to face up to the challenges of the order, to make mistakes, perhaps, to find new ways to build up our society, to keep and to be faithful to the values with which we founded our order; to the tremendous life that we live, the joy that brings to each and all of us in living out this way as a true disciple.

Has it been a challenge for you to pass on the leadership to somebody else?

No, not really, except that passing things on . . . it really means teaching a lot to the brothers. Showing them what is happening at this time. They have to learn the things that are going on in our institute. Show ways to go forward, governance, administration, deep prayer, the inspiration that comes from prayer, and all the wonderful things that God has given to us. They have to learn the needs of the future, the discipline that is needed, and the requirements for leadership in terms of communication while tirelessly seeking to help the poor, letting the Lord lead us without being afraid. Then, there are the matters of our rules, ministries, the reality of material things—water, life, cement, food, the everyday needs—lots of love, how to inspire one another, also to bear each other's burdens, sins, troubles, challenges, enemies, in all these matters how to conduct ourselves and how to move forward.

Does it worry you that the order might make adjustments, reforms as has happened in other orders?

Oh yes, sure, definitely; this is part of the life. I now just do whatever the Lord tells me to do: whatever I have to say,

I say; whatever I have to do, I do. I try to guide the brothers in a way of asceticism, self-discipline, and the love of the cross, while at the same time being very joyful and happy.

Is it fair to say that the Missionaries of the Poor were started by a Jesuit Priest?

Oh yes! I owe so much to the Society of Jesus! I learnt so much from them! The simplicity, the discipline, the concentration that is required to pray, to live together as one brotherhood, the call to give up everything, all those elements that I carried forward. In these days, much of that has been cast aside from the order; nevertheless, I got from the Jesuits the studies, the ability to identify the work of the enemy, the exposure to a very wonderful set of men tremendously gifted, well prepared, all these important matters that are part of my Ignatian background. All I learnt from the Jesuits and I carried forward.

Are there new challenges on becoming a Pontifical Order?

It is very subtle; we now report to the Vatican. Being elevated to Pontifical recognition, acknowledgment as "universal," means more pressure to spread, to move forward with confidence; we are now universal. We are called to live our life and continue being witnesses in the service of the poor. We would like to spread to more countries, but we need men and women well-formed, filled with humility and spirit of service, and at the same time joyful.

How would you like to see the order moving forward?

I would like to see more missions, more service, the order to be more ascetic but with a sense of joy. Take up your cross daily and follow me. Do not be concerned about the things of the world. Learn how to live together with a great sense of leadership and love, in self-sacrifice, in readiness to die for Christ, and hopefully grow in vocations with many, many more brothers joining us. We need workers in the vineyard, and we need men and women well-formed with true humility and spirit of service, committed and joyful at the same time. We have to take a step at the time. Keep working.

How are you going to pass on the music ministry?

Little by little, I need to find the right brothers to bring it forward. It is not so easy; it was a gift from God. It is in the process to formulate, find the right leadership. I have to pass it on; it will happen. It is not easy. I leave it in God's hands.

How should we, the lay Christians, live our faith in these modern times?

It is a difficult time. I think we have to be very bold to express the word of God. We are in an age of martyrdom. I believe that the people will be persecuted for living out the faith. Courage is needed; nothing matters but saying the truth. Once you do whatever you can, you know that God loves you. We need to speak the truth with love. We have to live according to the faith. We will have enemies, but we have to speak the truth. I would not be surprised that one day we will not be allowed to take children to our centers; people have already said that it is a waste of time. Sometime it is very discouraging, but we know otherwise that we need to be witnesses.

What did the Year of Mercy mean in today's church?

We need to recognize that we are all sinners, but nevertheless, we need also to remember that no matter what I have done, the Lord takes me back with all the mistakes. Sins are not okay, but we never condemn or hate anyone; we always love. But we need to remember that right is right and wrong is wrong. It is important to recognize the wrong. The Lord wants us to get up and start walking again. All of us have temptations; all of us know what is right and what is wrong. We will all come to the same conclusion, I have faith in that. We are all made from the same reality; we all know what is right and what is wrong and one day we will all reach the same conclusion.

How do you think we can better be a witness in the Church in this Year of Mercy?

We have to speak the truth boldly. We have to learn to carry the cross of Jesus. We need to be ready to suffer persecution, to face our sins and our weakness at all times, especially in this Year of Mercy. We need to forgive and accept forgiveness. Out of that will rise a Christianity that is truly humble and obedient to Christ. Take up the cross every day. We need not be afraid of suffering, not be afraid of sorrow, of weeping, tending the wounds of Jesus, purifying the wounds of Jesus of this time, in the suffering, in the dying, in the sins of people, in starvation, there you will find tremendous joy. We are called to be true Christians, to be Christ in the world and do it with tremendous love and joy; we know him. Pray. Pray how to know him better, how to love him more, allow him to love you, and to take you into his merciful love. There are many poor people to serve. There are more songs to be written. There is more good news to be preached, so I will still be around to chat and laugh with you and enjoy the happiness of serving God's kingdom here on earth!

Father Richard Ho Lung is a priest of mercy, a positive believer and thinker. He brings the love of Christ to the poor, facing the reality of good and evil with a positive faith, believing that the love of God has no boundaries. His thinking on mercy is in line with that of Pope Francis and Pope Benedict XVI who eloquently spoke of God's love in Deus Caritas Est: *"Life in God is like being immersed in a boundless ocean of love. No amount of sin, and no anxious clinging to lists of grievances, can overcome God's generous joy."*

Chapter Four

THE VISIBLE HEART OF JESUS

Most Reverend Brother Anil Minj, MOP

If a man loves me, he will keep my word, and
my Father will love him, and we will come to
him and make our home with him.

Jn 14:23

A new Superior General of the Missionaries of the Poor,
Most Reverend Brother Anil Minj was elected in March
2016 to take over the leadership of the Institute. His prefa-
tory comments are below, followed by an interview with him:

One day when I was young, I was playing in a vast open field in India, near my hometown with my younger brother. A large part of the field had been plowed and the rows were deep. At a distance we saw an old man in the middle of the plowed field, struggling to walk across the rows. He was falling and we realized that he would never make it across to wherever he might be trying to go. My brother and I looked at each other and I said, "Shall we help him?"

We ran across the field and reached out to him; we positioned ourselves by each side of the man and ask him to put his arms around our necks. We dragged him out of the plowed field to the flat part. We realized that he was quite old, very tired, and he was breathing very heavily. We were pleased that we had helped him, but unaware of where he was going, we kept on playing. Suddenly, I turned around to see how the old man was doing and to my amazement, I could not see him anywhere. In vain I kept on looking all around but he was nowhere to be seen. To this day, I keep that vivid image. "Who was he? How did he disappear? Was he Jesus in disguise? Was this a premonition from God that one day I would be called to help him in the needy?" These questions remain today in my mind.

The work that we do with the poor is extraordinary. We touch the sick and the suffering. At the beginning of my apostolic work, I greeted a leper and shook his hand. As I shook his hand, I realized he had no fingers. It felt like touching a strange creature, somebody out of this world. I was so frightened that I would catch the disease that my hand was trembling for a few days. Then I got convinced that nothing would happen to me, so I got over it. We have many children that come to us very sick, some with tuberculosis (TB), and we care for them. I was also afraid to catch TB; I eventually did. Thanks be to God, it was treatable and I recovered soon. God protects us in our work. We also take care of people with HIV; they are often chased out from their homes and their neighborhoods. They are very weak and dying in the streets. When we bring them to our centers, we administer medications to them and they recover. For some time, they do very well. We love them and accept them.

Brother Minj, please describe your family background.

I am from India, from a big family of six girls and two boys. My parents and grandparents were Christians. I learned from them the Catholic faith. When I was a young boy, I wanted to be a priest. We had a Belgian priest in our parish; his work and life attracted me very much and I wanted to be like him. When I was in the sixth grade, I joined the catechism classes. After high school, I went to college. Then, I expressed my interest in joining a religious order to my brother who was a Jesuit. He told me, "Don't worry, I will find a good community for you."

The MOP Brothers, Father Brian, and Father Hayden came to India; I was not able to meet them. They were going out of the room when I was coming in. My brother did meet them and told me, "I saw some nice missionaries here, would you like to join them?"

"It is fine with me," I said.

"It is a community newly founded in Jamaica," he explained. I thought Jamaica was in Africa.

Three days later, I saw Father Brian and he asked me if I would like to join them. I said, "I do." I didn't speak English and could not understand them quite well; I could get a few words here and there. I joined them in June 1993. I was then twenty-three years old. I spend the first year with them in India. We were building the monastery there. Our apostolic work consisted in feeding and administering medication to the lepers. After completing my first year in India, I was sent to Jamaica in 1994.

I started my novitiate in Jamaica. Corpus Christi was
then in development; we worked very hard in the garden
planting grass, flowers, and trees. We were seventeen brothers in the community and we didn't have yet proper training classes. We worked in Jacob's Well, Good Shepherd,
and the Faith centers. After lunch, we all had to work for
two hours gardening. It was enjoyable; we were few and we
knew each other very well. It was nice bonding and living
together.

Did you find the apostolic work hard?

No, it was not shocking to me at all. I came from a poor
family and so poverty was not unfamiliar to me. When I
came to Jamaica, I saw many poor people here. But the
work was natural. I had no fear of working with the crippled and sick, young or old people; I was prepared because
God had prepared me. I was intimidated, though, by the
Jamaican people—I found them huge—and by the way
they talked. Their culture was shocking to me too, and I
also found the way they dressed odd. In the centers I didn't
have any problem; I was young and found the work enjoyable. I didn't mind it at all.

Blessed is he who considers the poor! (Ps 41:1)

**Do you feel more connected to Jesus when you are
serving the poor?**

I do have moments when helping the poor I truly feel I
am serving Jesus. My parents prepared me for this work.

They were devoted Catholics and always told me, "When you eat, don't forget the poor; give to them whatever you have. Share with them." The words of his parents echo the teachings of St. Basil the Great: "The bread in your cupboard belongs to the hungry. The cloak in your wardrobe belongs to the naked. The shoes you allow to rot belong to the barefoot. The money in your vaults belongs to the destitute. You do injustice to every man whom you could help but do not."

My father would tell me bible stories. I was able to understand the Scriptures and relate them to things in life. Seeing people suffering was hard, but I understood, they [the sufferings] were there for our purification. I felt that God gave me the opportunity to serve him in the suffering. When I was a novice, I used to pray and ask Jesus, "What do you want me to do tomorrow?" I would sit by myself after praying the Rosary and talk to the Lord. He sometimes would not tell me anything, but I always felt very close to my heavenly Father. When we had forty days of prayer retreat, I felt that the Father was leading me to his Son. The Father showed me that Jesus is his beloved Son, and he wanted me to listen to him. I told the Father, "I will, but then, how will I go back to you? Because I love you very much."

I was struggling how to love in the same way the Father and the Son. Then, when I went into the chapel, my eyes were fixed on Jesus nailed to the cross. When I looked at his five wounds, I realized that he was my savior; he died and suffered for me. Looking at the cross, I felt the need to be very close to him and to serve him in the suffering. Through the Holy Spirit, I was able to immerse myself in

the mystery of the holy Trinity. We join hands together
and I could praise God, the Three in One. I realized that
the heart of Jesus is a symbol of that divine love which the
Redeemer shares with the Father and the Holy Spirit. The
heart of the divine Redeemer is the natural sign and symbol
of his boundless love for the human race. Jesus hanging on
the cross showed me that his heart was strongly moved by
different emotions: burning love, desolation, pity, longing,
desire, unruffled peace. The infusion of divine charity has
its origin in the heart of Jesus. I feel that the MOP are the
visible heart of Jesus, pouring his love onto the people we
care for.

**Do you see that whatever you do to the least of my
brothers, you do it for Jesus?**

Yes, sometimes in special ways. One day I was ministering to a boy in the Good Shepherd center. He had a
cyst in his neck full of pus. Whenever I took care of him
and dressed him, he felt so happy! He led me to feel that
I was doing God's work. I really felt that I was tending to
the wounds of Jesus while helping this sick boy. It was like
helping our Redeemer's broken body.

On another occasion when I was in charge of the Lord's
place there was one girl, Harper; she was crippled and
would be alone sitting in a corner. Every time I would pass
by, she attentively looked at me and kept her eyes fixed
on me. I could not figure out what she wanted and why
she was so persistently looking at me, but then I realized
that she might be hungry. So I went to her and asked, "Are

you hungry?" She could not talk and just kept on looking at me. I went to the kitchen and brought her some food. I was looking at her and feeling that she was somebody who really needed me. I felt like God was telling me, "I need your help." Whenever I would go by her, I would say hello, but she would not respond. I felt that God was there, looking at me through her eyes.

Do you ever ponder the mystery of suffering when you see these needy residents?

It is heartbreaking to see them suffering. As I look at them, I give thanks to God for my life. These children and adults are there suffering, but with a smiling face. They are like the suffering body of Christ. It doesn't make me sad seeing them, but they make me think of the beauty of God, and that He is asking me to purify myself through them. I feel that they are God's instruments to help me to get to heaven. They help me to obtain my salvation. God is really present in the suffering; we do what we can for them, we make them comfortable, and that makes them happy. I do feel compassion for them, but it doesn't make me sad. The world has to be evangelized through them and our doing this work. We care for them, and this is why it is so important for us to use the money we receive to help them. We cannot waste it in any personal things; it is for the needy. Our residents depend totally on us.

Can you recount some hard moment in your life?

I cannot think of any hard times in my life. God has blessed me in many ways. It is hard sometimes to adapt to changes in our own community. When I first came to Jamaica, we were only a handful of brothers. When I left Jamaica and came back later, we were many more. I had to adapt to the life of a larger community. But I decided to take the changes in a positive way. I focus on knowing that I am doing God's work.

Now I am the Superior General, and I do not have a hard time with it either. When they chose me to be Superior General, my first thought was, "Am I going to be able to do the job? Why did I say yes?" I was not ready to be Superior General. When I said yes, I cried. I cried because I accepted it.

The brothers asked me, "Why are you crying?" I was not crying for anything in particular. I prayed about it and I saw it as another opportunity that God gave me to grow and to serve him, and after that moment, I never felt fear anymore. I see it now as a gift. I realized that it is not a burden. It is a chance that God gave me to purify my own soul, to grow in holiness. I don't feel any more sadness or fear. I decided to be more enthusiastic. I look at my brothers to see what they need and what do I need to give to them. I talk to them about God, about the love for the poor. This is what I need to give them. It is not a burden; it is a challenge and a blessing. Life is always changing. I adapted to the bigger community and now to my new function as a Superior General.

How did your responsibilities changed after being elected Superior General?

I don't feel my responsibilities are a burden; I feel light. Some of the brothers are sometimes difficult, but when I see mistakes, I privately tell them, "Brother, this is not right." But I don't chastise publicly. I gently tell them that they have to change. They are respectful; the only thing that changed which I don't like is that they treat me like a king. Yet, I am one of them. I tell them, "Don't treat me any differently; I am just one of you."

> *Whoever exalts himself will be humbled; and whoever humbles himself will be exalted.* (Mt 23:12)

Are you going to change some things in the order?

I am here to lead our brothers to holiness. I don't want to change anything. I don't believe in changes of regulations or anything like that. I just focus on the life of the MOP. I focus more on working with love for the poor not so much as a social work, but a work of love. We have the expectation that not just the younger brothers but all of us, including Father Ho Lung, have to go once or twice a week to work in the centers, no matter whatever other job we might have to do. To work with the poor is our primary role. Even Father Ho Lung does it—not so much physical work, because he can't, but he is with our residents, talks to them; he does spiritual work. My main focus is love and work for the poor. Expansion is secondary. My first priority is to lead the brothers to holiness, to be Christ to others. The rules and regulations that we follow are strict but reasonable. We are happy with what we have. Father Ho Lung wrote everything; I have nothing to change. Father Ho Lung is always an inspiration to me. He is like a father figure to me. When I have questions, I ask him. Father Max Medina also gives me advice and when I thank him he is surprised that I feel very grateful, but I mean it. They all are an inspiration to me.

Will you start new centers in other countries?

We are working on opening new centers in Venezuela, India, East Timor, the United States, and Ireland. New vocations are so far growing. We had some problem in the Philippines this year, after new regulations took effect requiring that high school graduates add two additional years of tuition to their education. This has reduced the number of candidates this year. We have forty-five new vocations in India, thirty-five in Indonesia, and many more in Africa. In general, the vocations fluctuate.

How could the MOP more visibly witness to the world?

We reach out through our music ministry, the Internet, media, EWTN, and *Born and Blessed*, a program on the Jamaican TV that is on every morning, with Father Hayden and other brothers talking about the blessings of the Lord. Our work itself is an example to others. We also go to other churches; these various means are all good, but we don't have much more time.

What advice do you give the brothers when they come here?

God has called you to do this work. Don't focus on yourself; it is not about you but about your call, serving the Lord. By serving the poor, you serve God. If you reject [them], you are drifting away from the Lord. I do tell them to take their time before they say yes or no; this is a special call. If God has called you, say yes to the Lord. Some give excuses before they leave. I tell them not to use excuses to force their decision. The secular world is not bad as long as you are connected with the Lord.

The new Superior General, Brother Anil, is an example of simplicity, meekness, and love for God, for his brothers, and for the poor. He sees as his main mission to lead the brothers to God and to grow in holiness. He is not concerned for great things of the world, other than being a good and faithful servant of the Lord.

> *Let love be genuine; hate what is evil, hold fast to what is good; love one another with brotherly affection; outdo one another in showing honor. Never flag in zeal, be aglow with the Spirit, serve the Lord. Rejoice in your hope, be patient in tribulation, be constant in prayer. Contribute to the needs of the saints, practice hospitality.* (Rom 12:9-13)

Chapter Five

READY TO DIE TO MYSELF

Brother Johnson Talaban, MOP

*Come, O blessed of my Father, inherit the
kingdom prepared for you from the foundation
of the world; for I was hungry and you gave me
food, I was thirsty and you gave me drink, I was
a stranger and you welcomed me, I was naked
and you clothed me, I was sick and you visited
me, I was in prison and you came to me. . . .
Truly, I say to you, as you did it to one of the
least of my brethren, you did it to me.*

Mt 25:34-40

I was in my second year of MOP novitiate in Jamaica. I
was assigned at the Lord's Place in the AIDS section and
had to bathe one of the residents with AIDS. He was young,
in his mid-twenties, and he was laying down, very dirty and
smelly. He couldn't stand up or walk. I had to bring a wheelchair to take him to the bathroom; the stench was so bad,
that at first, I felt repugnance. My flesh was reluctant to do
the job, but my spirit was willing. I prayed to the Lord to
give me courage and show me his face. I carried the young
man to the bathroom. I cleaned, washed, dried, and dressed
him. When I was done, I looked at him, and I clearly saw

in him the face of Christ! I said, "Lord, it is you whom I served! You showed your face to me in this sick man!"

The resident said, "Thank you, brother!" I told him, "Thank you for allowing me to serve you." Seeing the face of Christ at that moment was a confirmation, a special revelation by Christ himself that I was serving him in the poor and needy.

Brother Johnson Talaban comes from the central part of the Philippines, Visayas, Guimaras Island. He joined the MOP in Naga. To travel there, he had to go to Iloillo, and from there to Cebu, which takes twelve hours, and from Cebu to Naga, another twelve hours. It is a day's travel by ship to Naga—a long trip for a young man of fifteen that had never traveled so far and was committed to give his entire life to God. When I talked to him, fourteen years later, he was happy and joyful, had never looked back or felt disappointment at his radical following of Christ; his journey is a continuous meeting with God and encounter with him in mystery and grace. As St. Pio of Pietrelcina said, "If the soul longs for nothing else than to love its God, then don't worry and be quite sure that this soul possesses everything, that it possesses God himself." Truly, speaking to Brother Johnson, one can sense God's presence in his soul radiating through his life.

Brother Johnson comes from a large and materially modest family. He is the eldest of nine children, three men and six women. His father worked in farming and his mother helped his father on the farm while taking care of her nine children. "We were a happy family; I give credit to my family for my vocation and upbringing. I come from a very devout, supportive, and simple family. My parents instilled the faith in me since I was born. When I was three years old, I was asked how Jesus died, and I opened my arms and crossed my legs to show how Jesus died. My mother was a very prayerful and religious woman. I owe my good Christian foundation to her."

When did you start becoming aware of your vocation?

I wanted to serve the Lord since I can remember, eight or ten years old; I did not know how, but I felt already a call from the Lord. One of my neighbors encouraged me to apply to a Catholic school run by the Sisters of Mary that offered free education and board to students coming from poor families. I applied, and by God's grace, I passed the entrance exam. There, these sisters continued fostering my desire to serve the Lord. The sisters encouraged me to be holy, to be a saint, and to do well academically too. Of all the subjects I had to take at school, I have to say that my favorite was religion. It was natural for me; I needed to learn more about my faith, and I treasured these classes. We had adoration of the Blessed Sacrament twice a week in the morning. I loved it. And we also had the Stations of the Cross. During the school time at recess, I would run to the chapel in the seventh floor just to say hello to the Lord and come back to the classroom. I really enjoyed it!

When Johnson was in his fourth year of high school, while playing basketball, he saw three brothers wearing white habits in his schoolyard. One of them was carrying a guitar.

"Who are these people and what are they doing here?" he thought. The loudspeakers announced that all the fourth year students were invited to come to the library to hear a presentation by the MOP. "I was hesitant to go, but something inside was pushing me to go." It was after all lunchtime, so Johnson went to the library in the second floor. There, for the first time, he would meet three very significant brothers in his future life: Father Brian Kerr, one of the first founding members of the MOP, Brother Augusto Silot, and Brother Marco Laspuña, the brother carrying the guitar. Johnson would later witness the death of Brother Marco Laspuña, who became one of the MOP's first martyrs on the day of Johnson's eighteenth birthday.

The brothers introduced themselves, explained what kind of work they were doing among the poor, and told the students that they were there seeking vocations for their order. After their presentation, they asked, "Who wants to become a missionary?"

The question shocked Johnson. "I will think about it! Maybe?" The brothers gave a questionnaire about basic knowledge of the Christian faith to all the students present. The last question was, "Would you want to become a missionary and why?" "I answered 'Yes,' and, 'Because I want to serve the poor.'"

Brother Johnson recounts, "Seeing them really encouraged me. The Lord really made clear to me that this was the community that he wanted for me. I was determined to join them. I had to finish high school first, but we corresponded and they kept encouraging me. Quite a few of my classmates responded too. The MOP sent a video to all the high school graduate students to watch, *Blessed*, a documentary of the MOP work and life. It struck me to see the people suffering with deformities, AIDS, and mental diseases. This was final, I was joining!"

The last day of school was family visiting day; Johnson's father was there, but his mother was not. "I told my father that I wanted to join the MOP. At first my father paused, was quiet, sad; then he said, 'If this is what God wants from you, go! You should do it!' It was painful for him; he had other dreams for me. I told him that I couldn't go home that year. He said, 'It is okay. Go!' So, I didn't see my mother. Papa said, 'I give you my blessing; do whatever the Lord wants from you.' I thanked the Lord for my parents, one of the greatest gifts the Lord has given me. They had been very supportive. I took the blessing of my father as a blessing from the Lord.

"We celebrated graduation in the morning and the brothers picked up the recruited students immediately after the ceremonies. Temptations came to me that day. We were called to the conference room. I didn't eat my lunch. I started having second thoughts about joining them, but a voice kept on telling me to go. After we all signed our names, we got the final graduation test results. I remember that day we sacrificed the school break time to pray the Rosary, do the Stations of the Cross, and spend time in adoration. The Lord was preparing us. When the time came to leave, we were ready."

After the first two weeks, the newly joined brothers were enrolled in the aspirancy period, which lasted around eight months; this was followed by their postulancy, when for the

first time they would take the habit. "When I was an aspirant, I already wanted the habit. One of the brothers told
me to persevere; my time to take the habit would come.
It was a little struggle during the formation. One day, my
formator told me, 'Your vocation is in danger!' I didn't
know what he meant. I spent the whole night praying in
the chapel, 'Lord, if it is your will let me stay, if it is not, let
me go.' Nobody picked me up the next day, so I assumed
that all was okay. My vocation had been tested."

His formation and work with the poor began in Naga.
After two years, he was sent to Jamaica in 2005 for his novitiate. The young Brother Johnson didn't know that new trials and challenges were awaiting him there. He adjusted to
the community life and apostolate work easily, but just one
month after his arrival, he would undergo another test. He
would witness the first loss of lives in his own community.
Brothers Suresh Barwa and Marco Laspuña [the latter had
gone with his guitar to recruit Johnson in the Philippines]
were shot to death at the center where he was doing his
novitiate. It was on October 27, 2005, after a farewell din-
ner for Brother Murray Goodman, who had been with the
MOP community for twenty years and had been assigned
to work in Uganda, Africa. Brother Johnson recounts, "I
started doing the dishes in the sink in the kitchen with the
other brothers, but I realized that I needed to clean the
refectory so I left the dishes and went out. Within a few
minutes, I heard gunshots, not unusual in Jamaica. But
then there was silence. I ran to the kitchen where I had been
washing the dishes. Two brothers were lying on the floor in
a pool of blood. Everybody was quiet, dumbfounded; we all

got down on the floor for fear that the assassin would shoot all of us. Brother Marco was groaning. And Brother Suresh was dead.

"Brother Marco died a few hours later, on October 28, my birthday. I had turned eighteen that day! 'God, Why?' I wondered. 'What does it mean that Brother Marco dies on my birthday?' Father Brian and Father Ambrose went with them to the hospital; the rest of us went to the chapel to pray in front of the Blessed Sacrament. Father Ambrose told Father Ho Lung, who was at Prince of Peace, of the tragedy. He ran back to our center. He asked us to get their blood and put it in a cup. He was sure it was the blood of martyrs. We put it on the altar before the Blessed Sacrament, and we prayed the Rosary; it was 4:00 a.m. We were all crying and singing. Father Ho Lung encouraged us not to be sad, to be strong. Their deaths in the eyes of the world were a tragedy; but in the eyes of God were a victory."

Did you ask, "Why not me?"

"No, I did not ask God, 'Why not me?' I thought the Lord had found them worthy."

Witnessing the death of two of their own did not weaken the brothers; they were strengthened and ready to follow the same path if necessary. Father Ho Lung asked the brothers the day after the murders if they wanted to stay in the monastery or go to work in the centers. All the brothers decided to go to work in the centers in the ghettos. This time they did not go by bus, but walked on foot through

the slums where the assassin lived to the utter amazement
of the people there that knew what had happened to them.

> We are afflicted in every way, but not crushed;
> perplexed, but not driven to despair; persecuted,
> but not forsaken; struck down, but not destroyed;
> always carrying in the body the death of Jesus, so
> that the life of Jesus may also be manifested in
> our bodies. (2 Cor 4:8-10)

At that moment, it didn't cross Brother Johnson's mind
or the minds of the other brothers that it was not safe there,
or that they wanted to leave. They indeed felt the source
flowing and carrying them onward; the grace of God had
strengthened them through this event. In confirmation
of Tertullian's statement, "The blood of the martyrs is the
seed of the church," vocations to the MOP grew exponen-
tially after this tragic event.

The brothers found out who the assassin was. They
started bringing food to his family, even though the assassin would sometimes give them an evil look. Within a few
months, the assassin was shot by the police in his own
neighborhood and taken to the hospital. Brother (Father)
Max went to see him at the hospital. He tried to hold his
hand but was rejected. He continued visiting him for several days and every time the assassin would reject his touch.
Just before dying, Brother Max saw him for the last time
and again reached out to him. The assassin finally broke
down in tears, without saying a word. The brothers believe
that he had finally repented.

Do you find it hard living in the community?

Times are rough sometimes when you live in this community, and once in a while it becomes heavy. Starting when I was an aspirant and continuing for seven years, I was trying to reconcile with a brother without success. I really prayed for reconciliation. It was tough for me. He didn't want to deal with me and it was hard for me. At times, I was really offended. He was my brother and I didn't want to keep grudges. At one point, I was almost about to give up, but I said, "No, I should not do that." I asked my formator to help, but he was not successful. The time came when this brother was going to be transferred. Just before he left, he said to me, "I am sorry, brother, for all I have done to you during all these years." I told him, "I already forgave you! Pray for me."

Community life is a cross, apostolic work is a cross, and even prayer sometimes is a cross. As St. Paul of the Cross says, "The soul whom God wants to draw to deepest union with him by means of holy prayer must pass through the way of suffering during prayer." Yet, from all these trials countless blessings and graces flow to me. When I am in desolation, I go to the Lord. There I find comfort and courage to carry on.

Even the residents are too demanding sometimes. It is too hard to work with them, especially when we cannot satisfy their needs, despite trying our best. One day, I called aside one of these complaining residents, "You have to understand, you are blessed to be here; we are here to bless you, you should be grateful that God brought you here." He said, "Okay, Brother," and he cried, "I am sorry, Brother, I know you are my son." It was a call to be patient and love them. On another occasion, a resident punched me when I was mopping the floor. He didn't want to be bathed and I helped another brother to hold him. I had left them and continued mopping the floor. When he passed by me, he hit me so hard that he left me totally breathless and pale. "Oh Lord," I said, "This is really amazing!" It takes patience love and dedication.

Another story from the life of the Missionaries of the Poor perfectly illustrates their devotion to God and the way in which they take Christ's words literally. The day was Good Friday. The brothers were rushing out of Bethlehem Center to go to the chapel upstairs to do the Stations of the Cross. Brother Johnson was following them when he saw a totally filthy man trying to roll in a broken wheelchair. In their rush, the other brothers kept on moving to get to the chapel on time. "Stop rushing! Christ is here!" yelled Brother Johnson. They went to the man, carried him to the bathroom, cleaned and washed him. He was filthy, full of urine and dirt, his clothes were torn, and they cleaned and washed him, noticing that he was very thin. They fixed his wheelchair, fed, and clothed him. He was very thankful for all that they did for him; he hadn't had a shower for six months, he told them. "I thought it was Christ we were tending to," says Brother Johnson.

Who gives you the strength to persevere?

It is Jesus himself who gives me the strength to persevere, the same Jesus that I meet through prayer and the sacraments. For ourselves, we can do nothing. From the grace of God we can do everything. Even prayer sometimes is hard; it feels dry, and we do not experience anything. It is another struggle. "Lord, you know I am trying to pray," and keep on praying without ceasing. Prayer is the source of my strength.

I believe that God's promises are true: "Come, O blessed of my Father, inherit the kingdom prepared for you from the foundation of the world; for I was hungry and you gave me food, I was thirsty and you gave me drink, I was a stranger and you welcomed me, I was naked and you clothed me, I was sick and you visited me, I was in prison and you came to me. . . . Truly, I say to you, as you did it to one of the least of my brethren, you did it to me" (Mt 25:34-40).

As I meditated on this passage when I still was in high school, my desire to serve the Lord grew stronger. I am happy, I have no regrets, I work, live, and carry the cross with joy in whatever way it comes. I give my life to God. I receive all the blessings from him. We receive immense joy and happiness that the world cannot give or experience.

Chapter Six

LIFE IS CHRIST AND DEATH IS GAIN

Brother Alfred Stephen, MOP

*Did I not tell you that if you would believe
you would see the glory of God?*

Jn 11:40

NOT all of us will have the opportunity to witness
the resurrection of a dead person, the parting of the
waters in the Red Sea, or Moses striking a rock and seeing it gushing abundant water. But Brother Alfred recounts
that he has seen the glory of God displayed in extraordinary
ways during his life as a MOP.

Brother Alfred was born in Chennai, a city in Madras,
in Tamil Nadu, a southern state of India. He made a special request to God through Mary when he was eight years
old, in a gathering of twenty thousand people during the
feast of our Lady of Lourdes. In this gathering, the priest
announced that when somebody writes a petition and puts
it in the cupboard, when the priest burns the petitions and
as the smoke rises up, the prayers are taken up to heaven
and answered. His mother told him, "Write your petition!"
He wrote that he would like to one day be a missionary,

even to the point of giving his life, that he would like to bring medicines and food to the people in the streets and fields, and to do whatever the Lord wanted of him. He later attentively looked at the smoke rising up, but shortly after that, he completely forgot about the smoke and his petition; understandably so, he was only a child.

> For I know the plans I have for you, says the Lord, plans for your wellbeing, not for woe. (Jer 29:11)

But the Lord did not forget little Alfred's petition, and he must have been preparing him to accomplish the wishes of his heart, expressed when he was a little boy. When Alfred was twenty-five, Father Ho Lung visited his hometown, Chennai, as he was looking into expanding his mission in India. Father Ho Lung asked Alfred if he would like to join him. Alfred asked, "What for?" Father Ho Lung explained to him that he was starting an order. Alfred thought to himself, "How can this man start an order? What does it mean?" Father Ho Lung asked him to show him places around his hometown and the adjacent town to recruit young men for vocations, so Alfred took him to local high schools around those areas.

At the end of the tour, Father Ho Lung asked him again to join them. Alfred told him, "Okay, Father." Before leaving, Father Ho Lung gave him a few dollars and asked Alfred to write or call him and consider joining him. Some time passed and Alfred forgot all about it.

Three months later, Father Ho Lung sent Alfred a ticket to go to Jamaica. "This is serious!" Alfred said. He didn't even know where Jamaica was. He went to see his parish priest who was also looking for an appropriate order for Alfred. Alfred told him that Father Ho Lung had sent him a ticket to go to Jamaica and join his order. The priest told him, "Might as well, if the ticket is here; get your passport ready." Everything fell into place quickly and easily. He got his passport and called Father Ho Lung. "Father, thank you for the ticket to go to Jamaica. What do you want me to bring?"

"Nothing, just come with an open heart!"

"What about clothes and other things I might need?"

"Nothing, just come with an open heart, but you can bring two pairs of clothes."

Never did Alfred know that two pairs of clothes would have to last him for over two years. Brother Alfred recalls:

After two years I went to Father Ho Lung and told him, "Father, I need more clothes!" He said, "No, two pairs of clothes are enough." I was not accustomed to wash clothes; my mother used to wash them for me. But by the end of two years, my clothes were tattered and raggedy. After washing them by hand every day, there was not much left of them. All we were doing was manual work; we had a simple life, no microwave ovens, no washing machines, and no machines to work in the garden.

Time passed and again I approached Father Ho Lung and told him, "Father, I want to go back home."

"Why?" he asked.

"I need more clothes."

"Clothes are not a reason to go back home; we can get them for you."

Another year went by, and my urge to go home continued: "Father, I want to go home."

"Okay, we can think about it."

After another year, I asked him again, "Father, what about now?"

"I am still thinking about it."

Five years had gone by since I had joined the order. By this time, I told him again, "Father, I really want to go home. You told me that after one year I could go home, and five have passed now." Looking back, I realize that he was afraid that if I were to go home, I would see my parents, they would persuade me to stay, and I would lose my vocation and would not return.

Finally, in the sixth year, he told me, "Well, it is time for you to go home."

"Time to go home, Father?"

"Well, I am trying to book your ticket."

"Trying, Father?"

"There is a way to do it; I am looking for another way. One way is to go to London, and from London to India. But," he asked, "Do you want to take your vows before you go?"

"I am not ready, but I would take them."

"Why are you not ready?"

"Well, I still find it difficult to wash my clothes."

"Oh, it is not a big issue," he said, "You can take your vows."

Six months later he told me, "You will take your vows tomorrow." They were not called vows yet, but promises, so I took my promises. Finally, Father Ho Lung said: "You can go home now. I have a ticket for you to go to London."

"Father," I asked, "What about from London to Madras?"

"When you get to London you will get the other ticket to go to Madras. Trust in God."

"How I am going to get it?"

"Well, you have to trust in God."

When I arrived in London, a priest, Father Campage, welcomed me. He told me, "You can stay, eat, and sleep here until I get you the other ticket."

"For how many days?"

"At least a week."

"A week?" I said, "Hmm, I will trust in the Lord."

I visited London and Oxford University and then I finally got my ticket and went to India. When I arrived in India, there were a few missionaries there and Father Hayden welcomed me. I told him, "What do you want me to do?"

"Nothing. Take care of the brothers."

"What about the other apostolic work, like feeding children, taking medicines to the sick, and visiting people in the slums?"

"Well, there is nothing like that here, but you can start something," Father Hayden said.

"Let me go to the ghettos and ask the children to see if they can come to the monastery."

"For what?"

"To eat," I said.

"Well, feeding them is good," he agreed.

I went to the ghettos nearby, Fatima Nagar in Poona, where we had our Christ the King Monastery. I gave the children candies. I asked them, "What do you want?"

They responded, "We want to eat breakfast."

So I went and cooked breakfast for them. I spoke to them using some words in English, and had somebody else to translate. I asked them to come every day. The next day there were twenty children. I asked them, "Are you going to school?"

"No; we do not have uniforms, we don't have books, and the school would not accept us," ten of them replied.

"Okay, let me see what I can do for you." So I went to Father Hayden.

"Father Hayden, I need some money."

"What for?" he asked.

"For buying books and uniforms for the children."

"How many of them?"

"Ten," I said, for the other ten were already in school.

The next morning forty children came to eat. It became obvious that I could not cook and feed all of them by myself, so I told Father Hayden, "We have to cook early in the morning to feed all these children. I need help from the other brothers."

"Okay, let us do it," he said. We cooked breakfast for all the children. These children were abandoned, living in the street, very poor, or orphans. They were very happy. I had them sitting on the floor, eating from leaves where I put some rice and sauce on the top, and the children were taking the food with their fingers, as we do it in India. I was

very happy seeing the children eating what I cooked and I
started praising the Lord for the happiness and joy I had
brought to them. After feeding, I started teaching them a
few things and singing a few songs.

The following days, there were about eighty children
coming to eat. I asked Father Hayden to assign three more
brothers to help me to cook and feed. He asked me, "Where
are you going to feed the children?"

I said, "On the floor."

Father Hayden insisted that I find a building. There was
a dilapidated and abandoned building nearby, belonging to
the diocese. I thought that perhaps I could ask the bishop
to let us use it. I asked and was given permission to use
it. I had to get the keys, so I wrote to the man who was in
charge of the building. He said, "There is nobody using it,
so nobody will stop you using it either. I would be glad that
somebody uses it and keeps it clean," and he gave me the
keys.

I was happy to see the children coming and eating inside
the building complex. They were all eating on the floor
when Father Hayden came by to see us. He said, "This is
very good, I am very glad to see the children eating, but
they cannot eat on the floor. We need to make tables for
them."

"Tables? That is a good idea. So the children will stand
up and eat from the tables."

"No, they need to sit down; we need to have chairs also."

"Okay, but I need money." Father Hayden gave me
money and we made wooden tables and chairs. I was
delighted to see children seating around the table and

eating. I took pictures and sent photographs to some people and to all the brothers. They were all happy to see them and told me that I had done a good job.

One day, a man came by and said, "Are you feeding the children and that's it? You are exploiting them! What about teaching them?"

"I don't have time to teach them." I said.

"So you are exploiting them," said the man. I was working really hard and feeding all these children and they were very happy. "What is the point of feeding them only? So they come here to eat and that's all?" he demanded. I didn't appreciate his remarks and that he would tell me that I was exploiting them.

That day, I went home very upset, thinking that maybe I should teach them, but how could I do that? I figured that the only way to teach them was sending them to school. The next morning I told the children that they needed to go to school. They told me, "Brother, we cannot go to school. Without eating we would be very hungry, and we have no uniforms and no books. The school would not take us in and if they were, they would soon kick us out."

The children were right; I realized again that I now needed real money to pay for all these things to send them to school. I asked Father Hayden, but he told me that we did not have enough—with the money that we had, we needed to support the brothers. He asked me, "What else can you do?"

I decided to go to schools to talk to the principals. I went to the schools and told the principals that we could feed the children and provide them with books and uniforms, but that we needed their help. The school principals were reluctant. They pointed out that it was going to be a waste of money; these children were poor and came from the low caste of our society; they had no support from their parents and they would not stay in the school for long. I assured the principal that I would take the responsibility, so after much negotiation, they offered us help with half of the cost of the tuition and asked us to pay for the other half. Father Hayden agreed, and we fed and sent to school two hundred children!

Then you will call upon me and come and pray to me, and I will hear you. (Jer 29:12)

It was a massive work. I got a group of brothers to help me feed the children before school. I was getting exhausted; we had to get up very early, at 4:00 a.m. I was very tired, but happy to see finally that the children were eating breakfast inside the building, sitting in chairs around the table, and going to school. However, my joy for our accomplishments was challenged again. Another man came by when we were feeding the children and told me, "You are wasting your time."

"How can you say I am wasting my time? I am feeding and sending to school all these children."

"You are religious, shouldn't you be also teaching them catechism?"

I thought about it and realized that he was right. But, how could I do it? I was tired and overstretched. I decided to call several catechists and pay them a small stipend, and so began to teach catechism to the children.

I had about one hundred twenty children in catechism, and after a while the children asked me to be baptized. I went to the parish priest and told him, "I have one hundred twenty children who want to be baptized."

He said, "Where are their parents? We cannot baptize them without their parents' permission and support. Besides, they are low caste; they don't need to be baptized, and it is a waste of time. They are not going to follow the Catholic religion. They are not going to be faithful and their parents will not follow up with them."

I was in shock! I told him, "Father, I will follow up with them!"

"And what will happen when you go away?"

"Father, this has been going on for years in the Church and the Church is still going on. We cannot deny baptism to these children!"

"Don't talk to me that way!" he said.

"Okay, Father, but it is the truth. I am working very hard in your parish, and you don't want to give me permission to administer the sacraments to these children?"

He said, "No!" and left abruptly.

> *Let the children come to me, and do not hinder*
> *them; for to such belongs the kingdom of heaven.*
> (Mt 19:14)

———

Brother Alfred does not take no for an answer, so as soon as he saw that he was going nowhere with the parish priest, he informed Father Hayden of what had happened and about his intention of seeing the bishop the next morning.

"The bishop?" said Father Hayden, "Do you think he is going to bother to talk to a simple brother?" But nothing discouraged Brother Alfred; he knew he was right and he was going to fight for these children.

Brother Alfred went to see the bishop and told him, "I am feeding all these children; I am sending them to school, and teaching them catechism. We are all children of God and the parish priest refuses to baptize them."

"I am very happy to see you feeding the children," responded the bishop, "What do you need?"

"I need to baptize the children."

"Who is stopping you? In fact, I am going to Rome and I need the names of all these children. I want to give a report to Rome about all the baptisms in my diocese."

Brother Alfred gave all the names of the children to be baptized to the bishop and got a letter from him with his permission to baptize them. He told Father Hayden. "Call another priest; we are going to baptize the children! I have a letter with the permission from the bishop."

All the children were baptized and made their First Communion. They all dressed in white. "It was a memorable and joyful event for the children and their proud families who witnessed it," recalls Brother Alfred. The following Sunday, all the parents and children came, and all the adults in the village, about five hundred, asked to be baptized. The parents were inspired and convinced by the goodness of the brothers who were feeding and teaching their children.

As he landed he saw a great throng, and he had compassion on them, because they were like

sheep without a shepherd; and he began to teach
them many things. (Mk 6:34)

Sheep without a shepherd, humble people marked as low caste by an unfair system and government rules, was what Brother Alfred saw in that village. He started educating the villagers and they all wanted to be baptized. He went then to Father Hayden with another request: "The whole village wants to be baptized!"

Father Hayden responded, "Be very careful; if you baptize them the government could close our mission. India is not very Catholic. The authorities can get mad at us and kick us out."

Brother Alfred realized the danger and proceeded cautiously, but was determined to carry out his mission. He started visiting the people in the ghettos. They were all poor and uneducated, belonging as they did to the Indian low caste. Brother Alfred asked them, "So, do you want to be baptized?"

"Yes, brother, but we have many statues of our gods."

"These are not gods! These statues have no use. You are worshiping false idols; they are not the real God."

"Brother, how do you know that?"

"I know. I worship the living God. These statues are useless. You need to throw your statues away if you want to be baptized."

"Brother, we cannot do that; the gods would kill us."

"Fine, I will throw them away for you."

"Brother, you cannot do that; they would kill you."

"It is okay."

"As I went deep into the village," Brother Alfred recalls, "I met a woman who had an anthill in her house, a huge hill made by ants. Inside the hill there was a snake that the woman and everybody in the village believed was a god. The lady would feed it milk and eggs every morning."

"What would happen if you were to stop feeding the snake?" Brother Alfred asked her.

"Brother, the gods would kill me."

"How can you afford feeding the snake? You are very poor and could use the milk and eggs to feed yourself and your family."

"Brother, I cannot do that. The snake would kill me and I would die."

"This is your home. Would it be okay with you if I destroy the anthill and kill the snake?"

"I would be glad, but the snake would kill you."

Brother Alfred asked for the help of the other brothers, and together they went to the house of this woman with claw bars and shovels to destroy the anthill. It was not an easy task, recalls Brother Alfred; the hill was made of hard mud, but together, they leveled it off to the ground. Brother Alfred went by the next morning to check with the woman. She was thrilled: "Thank you, brother! The snake didn't come back last night, but I slept outside the house just in case it would come to kill me."

The story spread throughout the village that Brother Alfred had killed the snake and destroyed the anthill. The whole village was convinced that their gods would kill him. But he continued challenging them: "I will come by tomorrow and throw away all your statues."

They said, "Okay, brother, but the gods will kill you for sure."

The next morning, Brother Alfred went by all the houses with a sack and removed all the statues. The villagers all panicked: "We cannot give you the statues, but you can take them. If we give them to you, our gods will kill us."

"Okay, I will remove them," Brother Alfred said. He took the statues under the scrutiny of the fear-stricken villagers.

"Be careful, they will kill you!" they warned.

He took the statues, put them in the sack, and dumped them in an empty dried well near his monastery.

The next morning, at 5:00 a.m., a group of people from the village went to the brothers' monastery. They were frantically pounding at the door. Father Hayden got up to talk to them.

"What happened? Is Brother Alfred alive?" they asked.

Father Hayden went to see Brother Alfred and asked, "What have you done to the people? They are asking me if you are alive. They are calling you. What have you done to them?"

Brother Alfred came out to greet them. They were very happy to see that he was alive. "Your God must be the true one!" the villagers shouted.

"Now that the condition of throwing away the statues and worshiping false gods is done, you can be baptized," Brother Alfred said.

"We want to be baptized!" they cried.

Brother Alfred started teaching them catechism and prayers. After some time, he went to the parish priest to tell him that the people wanted to be baptized. Again, he encountered stern refusal from the priest. "Brother, don't talk to me about it," the priest said, "This is a waste of time. These people belong to the low caste. Baptizing them would be a waste!"

As Brother Alfred did with the children, he was determined to baptize all these adults, so he went to see another priest. He told the priest, "Come and check to see if the people are ready and want to be baptized."

The priest came and said, "Well, some of them know their prayers, but there are some older people who do not know their prayers well."

Brother Alfred kept on teaching them, and eventually over five hundred people were baptized and received their First Holy Communion.

> *For as many of you as were baptized in Christ.*
> *. . . for you are all one in Christ Jesus.* (Gal 3:27,
> 29)

Brother Alfred's mission work did not end there. As he notes, "This was the first part of my five-year mission in India, where I also trained the young brothers doing their novitiate and taught them English. After India, I was sent to Jamaica for one year, and from Jamaica I was sent for six years to Uganda."

What happened in Uganda?

Uganda had many other challenges; life was very hard. There were mosquitoes that transmitted malaria, and the contaminated water frequently caused typhoid fevers.

Malaria stays in the blood for a long time; it stayed in mine for five years and the medications were not very effective.

In Uganda there was intense poverty. The brothers had no proper mosquito nets; they were either torn or missing. At night, they were so exhausted that they had no energy to even repair the broken nets. They were bitten by the mosquitoes, and they had to keep on working until they started getting a high fever and headaches. Then, they would go to the doctor who would confirm malaria and administer ineffective medication. Brother Alfred, like many others, did not develop immunity to malaria, so every year it came back again. This was not the only problem. The brothers not only were exhausted and sick, but they didn't have any water either. They had to get up at 3:30 a.m. and travel two kilometers to fill big drums and put them in the truck before the children and villagers would go there at 5:00 a.m. to get their water, so the brothers would not interfere with them. This went on for three months.

I started getting very discouraged.

One day after receiving the Eucharist, I told the Lord, "If this is what you call me for, getting up at 3:30 in the morning everyday, being exhausted, and getting malaria that is killing me, I give up. If this is what you call the brothers for, it is too much. I give up." After Mass, as I was going out, I saw a picture of the Divine Mercy. It was the picture of Jesus with the rays of living water flowing from his side. The picture was so bright that it moved me deeply. I said to him, "Oh Lord, you are the living water, you must be able to provide water for us, you control the rivers flowing into the sea. Why don't you give us the living water?"

Later that day, I saw a man in our monastery. I asked him, "Who are you?"

He told me that his name was Gabriel and that he was the father of one of our singers. He asked me, "What do you need?"

"I need somebody to dig a well for us to get water."

"Why are you asking me? Do you know that this is my profession, digging wells for water?"

"How would I know?"

"So, do you need water?"

"I would give my life for water—I am desperate!"

Gabriel explained to me that in the earth there is shallow water, and that by digging shallow wells, in some cases at only five feet deep, we could find water that we could then purify to drink. So he told me to start digging a well, five-foot deep with a six-foot diameter. I got other brothers to help me out. After digging five feet there was no water. I called Gabriel and told him, "We dug a five-foot deep well, and there is no water."

"Dig another five feet," he said. We dug another five feet with shovels and found four inches of water. I called him: "Four inches of water is nothing. What shall we do?"

He said, "Dig another ten feet."

"It is hard and difficult, but we will try," I told him, "What if we dig another ten feet and there is not any water?"

He asked, "Do you have faith?"

"Okay, we will try," I said.

After digging another ten feet, we found about two feet of water. I told Gabriel, "There is little water, not enough for a hundred brothers!"

He said, "Don't be afraid, and just dig a little more." We began digging deeper, which required taking the water out and working until midnight. In the morning, I got up early to look at the well to see if it was full of water. I found instead that all the soil around had collapsed, due to the humidity.

I called Gabriel again to tell him about the problem. He said, "Don't give up. Keep on digging more. Have faith."

It was a grueling task; we had to remove the wet soil and the water. We dug more, and finally the water gushed out. Now we need a pump. How are we going to buy it? We need money, but we don't have money to buy a pump! Dear Lord, help us!

In the morning, there was a call from a woman in England, Maggi. She informed me that some brothers were coming from Uganda and going to Jamaica, and they would be staying at her house.

"Very well, what can I do for you?" I asked.

"I need the names of the Brothers and passport numbers."

"I will send them to you."

"Where are you from?" she asked.

"I am from Chennai," I said.

"I am also from there and speak Tamil. Can I do something for you?"

"Yes, I am digging a well for water and need money for a pump."

"How much?"

"Two thousand US dollars."

"Don't worry," she said, "I will send them to you today."

"Oh, my God, this is what faith does! Truly, Lord, you never abandon us! You always give us what we need!" I had lived by then eighteen years as a missionary and I always had my prayers answered.

I told Father Ho Lung that she was sending the money, and Father Ho Lung said, "Go ahead; get the pump." We got the money and the pump. There was so much water that we could put three pipes into the street so the people around would get water too. There were about five hundred people getting so much water from our well all through the day that we had not much more left for the brothers.

I said, "We need to begin digging another well." So we began digging another well, and we got much more water than in the first one and at a much shallower depth.

From that time on, I never lost faith. During worship, I tell the brothers, "The Lord is a providential God. When he calls you to do something, he will also provide for you." I never cease telling the brothers about the Lord's miracles. He didn't just do miracles when he was on the earth. He does miracles everyday now!

Our monastery in Uganda was beautiful, built on a hill. The brothers had landscaped it beautifully; it was green like an oasis. The children would come every week to play on the grass rolling down the hill. We gave them water and food. We baked two thousand loaves of bread at night, and for that, we needed to get up at 3:00 a.m. We then served the children breakfast, consisting of bread and juice. This is what God wanted for us, to feed the people. The children came every Sunday and played drums during the Mass service. They were so lively that they would fill our hearts with joy.

After six years in Uganda, I came back to Jamaica. I worked with Father Brian and we were blessed by the generosity of many volunteers coming from the US and other parts of the world. We also evangelize through musical shows that we brought to Miami, New York, Rhode Island, Wisconsin, California, North Carolina, Trinidad, and other places. I also spent some time in North Carolina where we have a mission that ministers mainly to Hispanic immigrants; we give them food, teach them English and catechism, and provide them with a place to worship. We also administer to them the sacraments and take them to church.

How do you feel when visitors come to your centers?

When visitors come to our centers, they share for a week or two in our life. We have nothing, but we lack nothing. We have the vow of obedience, we are poor, we have no money, but they can see that we are happy. Some visitors complain that they spent a lot of money coming to visit and that we don't have many things that they like, like express coffee. I tell them, "Look, we have given all our entire life to live an austere life. I am sure you can sacrifice some of your material comforts for a week." Many others enjoy sharing our simple life and prayers very much. Many families come with young children, and they are very joyful; joy is our charism, living a joyful life. Even small children, some as young as three to nine years old, enjoy staying with us and want to come back again. They feel so much joy that they want to come back to stay with us rather than staying in a luxury resort and going to the beach.

[We are treated] as poor, yet making many rich;
as having nothing, and yet possessing everything.
(2 Cor 6:10)

Where are you going now and what are you going to do in your new mission?

I am going back to India in July. There is a group of sixty brothers in the mission of Orissa; we have a number of brothers that are getting ready to come to Jamaica. I will teach them English and music. I will also look for new conversions. This is something beautiful that the Lord asks me to do. One day, I might even have to give my life for God through persecution; this would not be loss but a gain. There is nothing else more important in my life than making my brothers happy, sharing my life with them, and sharing with them love of Christ and all the great things and favors that God has done in my life.

Is there the danger of martyrdom for preaching and converting people?

Well, I usually start feeding the children, then the parents are happy. When they see that there is no doubt about our way of life, then they come to us to ask to be baptized. Surely, we have to be very cautious. The government [in India] is against Christianity. We have to be very cautious; they could also close our mission. However, all this is not an excuse to stop us. It is the command of Jesus.

Brother Alfred is a man of faith and action. He lives his life fully rooted in the gospel; he travels the world evangelizing without fear. He says with St. Paul, "For to me to live is Christ, and to die is gain" (Phil 1:21). Thanks to Brother Alfred's tireless work, the bright light of the Risen Son, Jesus Christ, shines in many countries in the world, bringing joy and hope to the lame and the poor.

> *Who shall separate us from the love of Christ? Shall tribulation, or distress, or persecution, or famine, or nakedness, or peril, or sword? As it is written,*
>> *"For your sake we are being killed all the day long;*
>> *we are regarded as sheep to be slaughtered."*
>
> *No, in all these things we are more than conquerors through him who loved us. For I am sure that neither death, nor life, nor angels, nor principalities, nor things present, nor things to come, nor powers, nor height, nor depth, nor anything else in all creation, will be able to separate us from the love of God in Christ Jesus our Lord.* (Rom 8:35-39)

Chapter Seven
....

THE CANDLE THAT GIVES LIGHT TO OTHERS MUST ITSELF BE CONSUMED

Father Henry Lozano, MOP

*Let your light so shine before men, that they
may see your good works and give glory to your
Father who is in heaven.*

Mt 5:16

*F*ATHER *Henry Lozano is originally from the Philippines,
from the province of Camarines Sur. He is one of six children. His father (now deceased) was a photographer and his
mother a dressmaker. He was brought up in a home where
they loved, prayed, and respected God; his parents introduced him to the Catholic faith from birth. His home was
at a walking distance from the church. Both proximity and
exposure to the church and church activities stirred in him a
desire to become a priest.*

The pastor of my parish impressed me both by how he
lived his life and his commitment to his vocation. I was also
puzzled by the priests' lives because they were single and
still were happy and fulfilled. I wanted to discover what

inspired these men and what made them so happy despite
their single lives. From the age of six, I started thinking
about the priesthood, although I still didn't know what
it involved. I was impressed by their black cassocks and
wished I were like them. Then, I became involved in several church activities, and at the age of eleven, I became an
altar server until the age of sixteen. Then, I joined the choir
and a youth group, where I learned a lot about my faith.
My involvement in parish activities sustained my desire to
become a priest until the time that I had to make a decision, either to go to the seminary or to start a career. When
the time for the decision came, it was easy for me because
the foundation was already established, and my family was
very supportive. My parents were very happy to know that
one of their children was called to serve the Lord.

I graduated from high school at fifteen, and since I was
still young, I decided to enroll in political science at Ateneo
de Naga, hoping to finish and then enter the seminary. I
chose to go to college and graduate first, in case the path to
become a priest was to change. Things changed, however,
when I ran into a MOP poster that caught my attention.
The poster was unique and different from any other I had
seen before. It was written by hand in a cardboard, saying,
Missionaries of the Poor . . . Jesus needs you. The pictures
were real, pasted on the cardboard. In one of the pictures
there were two men dressed in white standing by a big garbage dumpsite, and they were surrounded by children with
unkempt hair, raggedy clothes, and by adults, scaveng-
ing in the garbage. These two men dressed in white were
talking to them and handing them food packages. The first

thought that came to my mind was, "What are these men doing in a garbage dumpsite?" I had never seen priests do this kind of work before. Yet, I thought they were doing the right thing, helping people. I thought that Jesus would have done the same while on this earth, because He was poor and reached out to the poor too. They attracted me, and I thought I would like to be like them and also work with and for the poor. What further struck me was that one of the men was black. I had never seen a black person before, and I thought that if he were black he must be from Africa. I thought to myself, "Wow! If he left Africa to serve my people, I should do the same." It turned out that the black man was Father Brian Kerr from Jamaica.

That poster left a lasting impression on me. I kept on pondering whether I should inquire about their community and join them. I told my parents that I would like to visit MOP at their mission house in Naga. They eventually took me there on January 1, 1995. We met with Father Brian and Father Max (then a brother). They spoke to me and to my parents about their community and their apostolate. After the conversation, they invited me to join them. The following day, after getting permission from my parents, I packed my clothes and joined them. It was painful leaving my family behind—it was especially hard for my parents—but it was also joyful to see a son leaving to commit his life to God in the service of the poor.

When I joined the community in 1995, I was inspired by the simplicity of the brothers' lives. They were living in a rented house with three bedrooms, and they were sleeping in bunk beds. What struck me even more was that

Father Brian would wear his habit while washing dishes and scrubbing kitchen and toilet floors. I also saw Father Max cooking and doing other very such humble tasks. I had never before seen priests doing this humble work, and this impressed me deeply because they showed me that they were really servants of the Lord, very Christ-like. The mission then was in its infancy. We had no apostolate ministry yet; it was something that was developed over time. I experienced their life as very fulfilling, joyful, and simple, but at the same time very strict. We were not allowed to go home, we could not go out whenever we wanted, we could not watch TV, and we had simple recreations like playing basketball scrimmage games outside or inside. I was the fifth to join the first mission in Naga; two more would join us later. Of the seven candidates that had initially joined, five left us, so only two remained. However, I was happy. I never entertained any kind of doubt about my vocation or about being in the wrong place. I knew I was in the right place, especially after seeing the example that Father Brian and Father Max had given to me. I just accepted that "many are called, but few are chosen." I was very grateful to God that He had called and chosen me.

What is the work of the Missionaries like in the apostolate centers?

The apostolic work of the MOP is highly challenging physically, mentally, and spiritually. The energy, zest, and selfless dedication of the MOP only can be fueled by divine grace that results from a closer encounter and deep relationship with the Lord. "The soul can feed only in God; only God can suffice it; only God can fill it; only God can satiate its hunger. Its God is absolutely necessary to it," said St. John Vianney. This relationship is only possible when we have Christ in our hearts; it requires his help and it requires his grace. For us men, it is humbling to do the kind of work that we need to do; we would rather be in the field working, doing manual work, but once we have said yes to the Lord we do whatever he calls us to do, and even though it gets to be a routine, there is always a freshness about it. We are aware that we are serving God, that we are taking care of Christ's broken body. It is a very humbling experience to be chosen to do this very special work, to tend to the suffering mystical body of Christ, like when Simon of Cyrene was asked to help Jesus carry his cross, or when Joseph of Arimathea got approval from Pontius Pilate to take down the body of Christ and prepare it for burial. Why me? Why I am asked to serve the Lord in this manner? He has chosen me and has given me the privilege to serve Him in the poorest of the poor. The service itself gives us joy. We experience real joy doing what we do. When we see the people happy, when we see the smiles on their faces, even though we have done something very insignificant—a small act of kindness, like bathing and lifting somebody up, or transporting them to their beds—they see it as an act of love and it means a lot to them. Handicapped residents often cannot do anything on their own. When you see them happy, you are happy. And even when they are not happy, we are still joyful; I still see the presence of God in them.

Can you tell us about your experience in Haiti at the time of the earthquake?

I had already been stationed at our Cap-Haitian Mission in Haiti for at least three years when the devastating earthquake of 2010 took place in Port-au-Prince. Then came that deadly cholera outbreak towards the last quarter of the same year; this was one of my most challenging tasks I have ever had to handle, but it also one of the best and deepest experiences that I have ever lived because it took the best of me. We worked day and night trying to save the lives of our residents, helping them to survive without counting the cost. We had to work long days and spend sleepless nights. At the end of the day, I would feel really happy because, with the help of God, we had saved lives.

I saw residents before my very eyes that were falling into this ravaging disease, some of them very old and others young, including the crippled children. We tried to tend to these residents during long hours every day. We would not neglect our prayers, but would still begin our day early in the morning with Mass and prayer, eat a little, and rush to the centers to make sure we would help those infected. It was a very challenging time; we were constantly occupied in replenishing bodily fluids in those infected and also trying to prevent the infection from spreading to the healthy ones. We had to chlorinate the water and wash our hands and the hands of the residents, and clean the toilets with bleach thoroughly. On several occasions, I personally had to rush residents who became infected to the hospital. We frantically worked trying to save lives. Yet, in the midst of this distressful time, I felt as if the Lord had covered us with his presence; I felt like he was truly pleased [because] even though we were overburdened, overstretched, [we] never thought of ourselves.

On one occasion, as we were pouring ourselves out, it was really hard. I took five children to the hospital at one time, and one of them did not make it. As soon as I reached the hospital, and as I was standing there, I tried to rehy-drate by mouth one of our residents, a young girl, while the nurses were frantically looking for her veins. They could not find them. As her life was slipping away, I felt that I could do nothing else to save her. I broke down in tears; it was one of the few times that I really cried. I said, "Lord, please spare this child, spare her life." He did not. We had to have faith, God was there. We have to accept the plans of God even when we don't understand them!

> In this you rejoice, though now for a little while you may have to suffer various trials, so that the genuineness of your faith, more precious than gold which though perishable is tested by fire, may redound to praise and glory and honor at the revelation of Jesus Christ. (1 Pt 1:6-7)

When I came back home, I was exhausted but I went to pray in our chapel. I was close to offering my life for the sake of these children, if God saw it fit. Indeed, I was almost ready to offer my life to him if only this ravaging disease would stop! But right there and then, and as an answer to my prayer, I felt the real presence of God enfolding me. An immense sense of peace overshadowed me; it was like God had given me an embrace saying, "Everything will be okay. All will be well."

I remained in Haiti from 2006 to 2011. With my team of brothers, we helped the survivors of the earthquake with food, mobile clinics, and took in displaced people, housing them temporarily until we found low-cost housing for them, so their children could go to school. I would have liked to stay longer, but then I was sent to lead the mission in Uganda.

Could you recount some other experiences from your work that highlight the value and dignity of each individual?

Yes; Paul Frazer was a young man with Down syndrome that we were caring for at Faith Center. People with Down syndrome are often considered not to be very conscious of their value, or maybe that they are not capable of self-sacrifice or of feeling compassion for others. But I experienced otherwise. Indeed, they proved to be very caring and compassionate. One day, after the brothers and I had finished work at Faith Center and were having snacks, Paul was around us. When I got my share of a cake, I gave him half of my portion, expecting that he would eat it. To my surprise, instead of him eating it by himself, he looked around and divided it among the other residents. I was in awe to see that even people like Paul are capable of self-sacrifice for the love of others; they are aware that others have feelings and needs too.

I saw it again in another Faith Center resident, Christopher. Christopher was partially crippled and very sensitive. I remember being asked to clean the floor of our chapel in the Center. As I was doing the work by myself, sweeping, mopping, and dusting, I turned around and noticed that somebody else was helping me. I was pleasantly surprised to see that Christopher, with just one functional hand, was mopping the floors with me, even though I never actually asked him. He simply saw me there and reached out to help me. This is the life of MOP—we reach out to the needy and they reach back to us. From this time on, the residents inspired me to give myself even more generously.

Do you ever feel unfulfilled when you cannot attend all the needs of the poor?

It breaks my heart not to be able to provide everything they need. But we do what we can. And even if at times all we do is to simply listen to them, it relieves them of their burdens. These people go home knowing that somebody has listened to them, cared for them, and given them an opportunity to pour out their heart. We have to let go and let other people who have the means address their needs.

Of the four vows that the MOP profess, which vow is the most difficult?

Obedience in general is the most demanding. Obedience is difficult because there are certain things that we wish to do our way without necessarily having to listen to anybody else. Obedience requires submission of our will to the will

of others and to the rules of the Order. It is demanding and
can be very challenging at times. Free service to the poor
does not bother us; we love to help them without counting
the cost. Poverty doesn't bother us either; we enjoy having
less rather than more, it makes us free. Chastity is not too
difficult either, because our own brothers surround us; we
support each other and we get encouragement also from
the residents that we consider as our families. Sometimes
we might miss having our own biological children, but we
have many children in the centers that are our children too.

**Do you ever feel anxious thinking about where the
funds are going to come from?**

It never bothers us, and certainly not me personally. From
my experience of being in charge of missions, I always saw
that God provided abundantly to meet our needs. I never
worried about how we were going to go through the day
or if we were going to have enough. God was always there,
seeing our needs and providing for us. The key is to remain
faithful. People are always moved to share their resources.
If we start cutting corners, the Lord would not be pleased
and the people would not be moved to give. I believe that
the Lord will always provide.

Can you tell us something personal about yourself?

Something I am grateful to MOP for is our vision as
we embrace this life. As long as we cling to the vision, we
believe we are on the right track. Our vision is that every
human being, regardless of their circumstances, is precious

in God's eyes. It is what we try to impart in our Centers and to the whole world. As long as we are faithful to God and remember that "As you did it to the least of these my brethren, you did it to me" (Mt 25:40), we know we are on the right path. For those who remain faithful, we are certain that what He promises is true: "Come, ye blessed of my Father, enter into the kingdom prepared for you from the beginning." I see our work as a direct shortcut to heaven; the works of mercy are a shortcut to heaven. Jesus' message is very clear, "It is me myself whom you gave a drink, it is me myself whom you fed, it is me myself whom you clothed," and this is really our vision.

How does the vision of the MOP contrast the vision of the world?

The world has become diverted in its focus. We see our worth in our possessions, and in what surrounds us, but in truth, as the Beatitudes say, "Blessed are the poor in spirit, for theirs is the kingdom of heaven" (Mt 5:3). The poor are the happy ones. Happy means having the Lord. If we do not have the Lord, even though we may have all the material things, we are not satisfied. I wish the world could see this. It is in Christ alone that we find true happiness. Therefore, we need to have witnesses, we need to have Christians truly in love with Jesus. Once the secular world sees how fulfilled Christians are, they will begin to think and ask themselves what makes these people so happy. Like the early Christians, the pagans were so puzzled by them because, despite the fact that they were persecuted and put to death, they were still happy, singing praises, and there was no anger in them. Also because the charity that the Christians showed to others was striking, the pagans wanted to find the secret of their happiness, which they were not able to find until they embraced Christ themselves. As St. Charles Borromeo said, "The candle that gives light to others must itself be consumed." Thus, we also have to act. We ourselves need to be consumed to give a good example to others.

A new commandment I give to you, that you love one another; even as I have loved you, that you also love one another. (Jn 13:34)

Brother Alfred, far left, with Orissa MOP Family

Brother Anil Minj

Brother Paulo Llarena

Brother Prasant

Brother Johnson Talaban with resident

Above: Brother Spo Omolo
Left: Brothers at Corpus Christi welcoming visitors

Frs. Hayden Augustine and Brian Kerr, Founding Members

Above: Fr. Henry Lozano
Right: MOP Novices in training, Corpus Christi

Fr. Richard Ho Lung

Chapter Eight

MY BROTHERS ARE MULTIPLIED

Brother Dexson Melchor, MOP

A big sign greets the visitor: *Mount Tabor where Heaven and Earth Meet.* Indeed, this place is magnificent; the vegetation, gardens, and the 360-degree view of the mountains of Jamaica are breathtaking. Two groups of brothers live there, one tending the farm and caring for the children in the Beatitude Home, and the second studying and praying in preparation to receive their final vows.

Mount Tabor Monastery was built in 2004 after the MOP received a gift of several acres of land in the mountains of Iron River, north of Kingston. In the summit of the mountain, named Mount Tabor, a beautiful retreat center for visitors and the brothers, and a residence for disabled children, the Beatitudes Center, was built. There, the Brothers also created a small-scale farm with pigs, rabbits, sheep, cattle, and chicken.

As I was sharing a simple breakfast with eighteen MOP at Mount Tabor, we marveled at the presence of the universal Church in their very own dining room. In that room there were fifteen brothers and two visitors representing five continents. The message of Jesus, "Go into all the world and preach the gospel to the whole creation" (Mk 16:15), was being fulfilled in our midst. The MOP come from all the corners of the world, heeding the command of Jesus: go and preach the good news through all the earth. They are all united in one faith, one love, and one mission: "Joyful service with Jesus on the Cross."

As we were sipping coffee, Brother Dexson, sitting by my side, shared his story with me. He came from a very poor family in the Philippines; he was the youngest of seven brothers with limited access to education or material goods, yet they were a happy family. I remembered him as the smiling brother; he can be recognized by his big smile. I find him to be a beautiful and deeply meek, simple, and humble person. He had been assigned to work in the mountain and take care of the livestock and farm, and he loved being there.

One day, Brother Dexson was feeling unworthy of being part of a very holy and talented MOP community, and realizing that he had no special skill or talent to offer made him very heavy of heart. He approached Father Richard Ho Lung and told him, "Father, I came to serve the poor, but I am poor myself, and have nothing to offer to God or our community." Father Richard Ho Lung, gently looking at him, told him, "Brother, seek first the kingdom of God and all these things will be given unto you."

Brother Dexson's face lit up again with a big smile when he recalled that moment and rejoiced in the encouraging words he heard from the founder of his Order. Brother Dexson's simplicity enriches the people who come in contact with him.

Brother Dexson joined the MOP when he was eighteen years old. His vocation story was simple, as is often the way with God's plans for us. Two MOP walked into his home in the Philippines one day. They were visiting his parish, and his mother asked them to visit her home. The MOP asked Dexson, "Do you want to join us?" He heeded their call and took a long trip by bus and by ferry to attend the "Come and See" retreat. There, he found that God was calling him to serve Him in that community. When he came back home, he told his parents and brothers that he wanted to be a MOP, and left to join them.

His mother was a very faithful and loving woman who prepared him to become a MOP; she taught him all the prayers and practices of the Missionaries. She attended Sunday Mass, prayer, and the Rosary. His mother taught him also how to take care of himself, cooking, cleaning, and sewing. "There was hardly anything new I learned or that was hard for me to adapt to when I joined the MOP," he recounts. His mother, he says, was "a pre-MOP" for him.

When Brother Dexson joined the MOP, he embraced his new family. He recounts that he did not miss his family so much; he had six brothers before, and now he says his brothers have multiplied. He felt at home with the MOP, even much happier than in his own home.

He was assigned to work in the mountains with another group of other brothers. There they live, worship, pray in community, and take care of the livestock, as well as a small farm which provides enough food for them and for some of the other communities.

Brother Dexson loves being in the mountains. He shares,
"I prefer to be in a peaceful place like the mountains. When
I am with the sheep or the other animals, I remember Psalm
23:

> *The* LORD *is my Shepherd, I shall not want;*
> *he makes me lie down in green pastures.*
> *He leads me beside still waters;*
> *he restores my soul." (Ps 23:1-3)*

When he sits down and looks at the surrounding beautiful nature, he remembers Psalm 8:

> *O* LORD, *our Lord,*
> *how majestic is your name in all the earth!*
> *What is man that you are mindful of him,*
> *and the son of man that you care for him?"*
> (Ps 8:1, 4)

Or Psalm 148:1-4:

> *Praise the* LORD *from the heavens,*
> *praise him in the heights!*
> *Praise him, all you his angels,*
> *praise him, all you his hosts!*
> *Praise him, sun and moon,*
> *praise him, all you shining stars!*
> *Praise him, you highest heavens, and you water*
> *above the heavens!*

Brother Dexson says, "I live every day and every moment
in the presence of God, blessing him and thanking him for
so much happiness and joy that he has bestowed upon me."
Well, where is the poverty when you live all day in the presence of God?

Blessed are the poor in spirit, for theirs is the
kingdom of heaven. (Mt 5:3)

Mount Tabor is truly a foreshadowing of heaven. Living day and night in simplicity, freedom, and in the presence of God: this is the life of the MOP; this is the life of the smiling brother, Brother Dexson.

Brother Dexson lives in perpetual simplicity, not looking for things too sublime for him; his soul is stilled and quieted in the presence of God. He heeds the words of Jesus: "Unless you turn and become like children, you will never enter the kingdom of heaven" (Mt 18:3). He is like a child, living a life full of love and happiness in the loving presence of God in nature. And, as St. Teresa Benedicta of the Cross says, "Holy realism has a certain affinity with the realism of the child who receives and responds to impressions with unimpaired vigor and vitality, and with uninhibited simplicity." This is the life of Brother Dexson.

> *Praise the LORD from the earth,*
>   *you sea monsters and all deeps,*
> *fire and hail, snow and frost,*
>   *stormy wind fulfilling his command!*
>
> *Mountains and all hills,*
>   *fruit trees and all cedars!*
> *Beasts and all cattle,*
>   *creeping things and flying birds!*
>
> *Let them praise the name of the LORD,*
>   *for his name alone is exalted;*
>   *his glory is above earth and heaven.* (Ps
>   148:7-10, 13)

Chapter Nine

MINISTERING TO THE SUFFERING CHRIST

Brother Marc Maurice, MOP

I say to you, you will see the sky opened and the angels of God ascending and descending on the Son of Man.

Jn 1:51

"WHEN I was working at Jacob's Well, one of the residents was dying. I was by her side comforting and praying for her. She could not talk, but then, I realized that her face lit up and she was trying to communicate something to me. Suddenly, she looked at the ceiling and said, 'The angels are here, look how beautiful they are!' I looked up where she was pointing, I could see a very bright light, but I could not see the angels. I was so moved that I called another brother to witness it. We continued praying by her side. After a few minutes, she passed away."

Brother Marc is from Haiti. He was in elementary school when he felt that the Lord was calling him, but he could not discern yet what kind of call that was or what it meant. He shared it with a priest, who told him to pray about it. But even when he was praying, he wasn't sure what he was praying for. Eventually, it became clear to Marc that his vocation was to be a missionary. When he told his parents, they were not happy about it and did not encourage him. Lacking the support of his parents, Marc told his parish priest that he wanted to become a missionary, but he didn't have the backing of his parents. The priest told him that since he was an adult, it would ultimately be his decision and asked him to keep on praying about it. He recounts, "The Blessed Mother was key in my vocation; she led me to her Son." After some time in prayer and discernment, Marc told his parents that he had decided to become a missionary. "If that is what makes you happy and what you want to do, go ahead and persevere," was their response.

The MOP had just arrived in Haiti in 1995. Marc was in high school and had seen their brochure with their contact information. One day, he decided to visit them. He talked to them about his situation and intention. The brothers invited him to stay and join them. It seemed to be the community for him, so Marc decided to stay with them for some time. He then went back home for a year to think if this would be the type of life he wanted to live.

"As I reflected about what I had seen and experienced, I decided that maybe this life was not for me. I was not attracted to their apostolic work, seeing how the people they were caring for looked like; the smell and the hard work of the MOP was not appealing to me. I kept on praying about it while I was home for an entire year, and the Lord kept on calling me to go back. I understood that the Lord was truly calling me to be a MOP. I then decided to give myself to the Lord completely and to join them. I stayed in Haiti for one year before I was sent to Jamaica. There, I continued my formation, postulancy, and novitiate.

"It took me sometime to learn English, to get immersed in the community, and to understand the cultures. After my postulancy, I spent two years in the novitiate before I took my first vows, and then I was sent to Uganda. Uganda was a very good experience for me, a place of spiritual growth and commitment. It was a small community, so it was easier to adapt, to get to know each other, and to get adjusted in the community. The challenge of learning a new language was very tolerable. Initially, we did not have a center; we rented a house for one year. Four months later, the local bishop gave us permission to construct a house on a piece of land that was given to us, so we built a center and started the apostolic work. I remained there for five and half years, where we took care of our residents and looked for poor people in our surrounding areas. We would visit them and help them with water and food. When I left Uganda to come back to Jamaica, in 2006, I left behind fifty African brothers. The number of residents grew also from one hundred to two hundred now."

Where do you get your zest for your daily work?

Our motto is "Joyful Service with Christ in the Cross." To be united with Jesus on the cross is our call and commitment. Prayer is key. We have Mass, adoration of the Blessed Sacrament, and prayers from the rising of the sun to its setting; even during the work hours, we stop to pray. This helps us to stay connected, to get through the day.

Our strength comes from God who pours His graces on us and strengthens us. Living in community also helps to encourage each other. There are also key experiences with the residents that touch us deeply. My experience with a dying woman who had a vision of the angels just before she died, and other experiences with the residents that we meet in the centers are special moments of grace that remind us that we are in the presence of God, that we are serving Jesus himself in the poor and neglected.

These special moments of grace or visions occur in special circumstances, but when they do, they leave a deep impression on us and remind us that we are truly serving the Lord. I remember when I arrived in Jamaica and was assigned to Jacob's Well. I had another experience that reminded me once more that by serving the poor, we serve God. Near our center, there was a lady dying in the street. We saw her; we were not sure what happened to her; she could not speak, and so we could not find out what her name was or where she came from. We brought her to the center; we laid her down in a bed and gave her water; suddenly, she looked up to us and said, "God bless you, brothers!" and she passed away. These were her first and last words. This reminded me of the words of Jesus: "As you did it to the least of these my brethren, you did it to me" (Mt 25:40). To help a dying person and hear from her mouth just before she went into God's presence, "God bless you, brothers," was truly comforting; it was a blessing from God. Blessing us, she went to the Father. As MOP, we are ministering to anyone in dire need. We believe that whosoever we minister to is another suffering Christ; all represent Christ, there is no particular

person who is more or less like Christ. We serve in all of
them Jesus himself.

Are there moments of doubt in your life?

Sometimes, we can feel moments of doubt, moments
of discouragement, but God always sees us through these
darker times as if he is letting his light and grace shine
through the clouds. When we see all the young brothers
coming full of joy and enthusiasm, they remind us that
we are in the right place. When our order was elevated to
Pontifical Institute, it was yet another assurance that we are
in the right place. It assures us that our life as MOP is recognized by the universal Church as a way to sanctity. We
do sometimes think of the allures of the outside world, but
we reject them as a temptation. We think of the vows we
have taken for life and we are committed to them. This is
our life, and it is a life of sacrifice, a life of union with Christ
on the cross, and it is there where we find our joy and happiness. The world has completely different standards that
at the end fail to satisfy; in the MOP, God fulfills us with
everlasting gifts.

Which of the vows is most difficult to live by in the life of a MOP?

The most difficult is obedience. It is hard to give up your
will; we like to be in control, but we have to renounce our
will; we have to renounce ourselves. We are sometimes
selfish, but we have to give up our desires and be humble. "Unless a grain of wheat falls to the earth and dies, it

remains alone; but if it dies, it bears much fruit" (Jn 12:24); we have to die to ourselves so our fruit will be plentiful. We go to God in our need; we go to God in our weaknesses; we go to God in our thirst. God never disappoints us and never lets us go empty. As Jesus says, "If any one thirst, let him come to me and drink. He who believes in me, as Scripture has said, 'Out of his heart shall flow rivers of living water'" (Jn 7:37–38).

What are the new challenges with the Pontifical status of your order now?

My dream is to extend the mission to other parts of the world; we need to evangelize and to witness that God is alive in our world now. We need to live our life in selflessness and in witness to others. We are followers of Christ and need to give others example with our lives. We have to heed the call of Jesus to "Go into all the world and preach the gospel to the whole creation" (Mk 16:15). We need to be witnesses of the love of Jesus over all the earth, but we need more vocations too. As Jesus said, "The harvest is plentiful, but the laborers are few" (Lk 10:2). We pray every day for an increase in vocations, asking God to send us more laborers to work in his vineyard. The people need to feel something new in us; they need to want to live the Beatitudes. When we hear Jesus' call, we follow him. We are encouraged by many new vocations, coming mainly from Africa, the Philippines, and India. It is for us to go there and proclaim the truth because the world is hungry for the truth. We invite them to our program "Come and

See" that lasts for two weeks. We bring them to our centers to experience our life. God does the rest. My desire is that young people come here and share in our life. I wish and pray that young people are not afraid to say *yes* to God. They should not be afraid to say *yes* to Jesus, to follow him; they lose nothing. They gain everything.

What is most remarkable about you?

I am happy to be a MOP. I found Jesus in my work and in my life and I am totally committed to serving Him. I am joyful and approachable. I am always ready to pour myself out to support others. It is always very important for us to have somebody to be there for us. I am here for others, and I also need others to walk with me too. We have excellent leadership and we are always available to lead others. We know and have the assurance that whatever might happen in the world; our order and our mission will go on.

Are you ever worried about how are you going to get enough food to feed all your residents?

In our constitution, we believe in Divine Providence. Sometimes I wonder on the ways of the Lord, on the way he is going to provide for all, not so much whether he will provide. But I have to trust in him that he will always come through in his unexpected way. I know that it will happen. I do question sometimes how and when it will happen; it is my human side. God provides in the most unexpected ways and it is for us to totally trust that he will do it in his own way and in his own time. "Cast your burden on the LORD,

/ and he will sustain you" (Ps 55:22), and this is what I am always learning to do in total trust and surrender.

As St. John Paul II said, "Man is in the middle between God and nothingness, and he must choose." Brother Marc has said yes to God, he has chosen to follow him, and his cup overflows.

Chapter Ten

BROKEN BREAD TO BE
GIVEN TO OTHERS

Brother Rodrigo Landong, Jr., MOP

*My grace is sufficient for you, for my power is
made perfect in weakness.*

2 Cor 12:9

"I was born in the Philippines, in a village around forty minutes from Naga, to a large family, five boys and five girls. Two died, and now I am the sixth of the eight children. We came from a poor family. My mother was a housewife and my father was the main breadwinner, the provider. My mother sold charcoal in the market to make some money to help us to go to school and study. When I was a little boy, I saw my mother and father struggling. The money from charcoal was not enough to sustain us. My older sister and brother also helped to take care of the family. I also helped selling charcoal in the market when my parents were sick. There was no sense of shame from helping my parents doing this humble work. My mother also cooked some snacks that I would sell at school to help with some money. I felt the responsibility to help my family

103

in any way I could. From this humble beginning, God was preparing me for a life of service to him.

"When I was young, I was very sick after contracting hepatitis B. The doctor told my mother that I would not survive. My mother was very upset and faithfully prayed for my recovery. She had lost two children already and didn't think she could take losing another one. She made a promise to God that if I would survive, she would dedicate me to serve him. She never told me that. But after recovering, and when I was eleven years old, she took me to church to serve as an altar boy. Then, she told me about the promise she had made to God. As a young boy, I did not know anything about religious life. For me, being an altar boy was enough."

When did you first discern your vocation?

My parents were strong Catholics. My mother taught us about faith, about the Lord, and always sent us to church. Seeing a priest celebrating Mass, and especially during the consecration, I felt something special, and I always said, "I want to be something like that." Not necessarily becoming a priest, but I wanted to be like the Eucharist, broken bread to be given to others. The thought of serving him came out later when I was in the fourth year of high school. As the graduation came closer, I remember asking the Lord, "If you want me to serve you, show me the way." I didn't know about religious life. I only knew there were priests and nuns. I didn't necessarily want to become a priest, but I wanted to serve the Lord. I said, "Lord, I want to serve you but I do not know where."

In the remaining months before I graduated from high school, the MOP brothers came to our school for a vocation campaign. They told us about their mission and life; I was inspired by their work. I realized that this was exactly what I wanted to do and what the Lord was calling me for. I was a little disturbed about their white habits as they seemed a little odd. I thought they were women's dresses. The brothers gave us a date for a vocation seminar that I was not able to attend because of school activities. Instead, I planned to go to Naga City, where the brothers have a mission, only forty-five minutes by bus. I told my parents of my plan and they accepted it and my sister promised to accompany me. However, the day I was supposed to go, everybody let me down; they thought I was joking. I was disappointed with all of them. That day I had one hundred pesos and decided to go alone without anybody's help, although I was afraid to travel alone. I skipped lunch and came back home late, just to show my family how bad I had felt and never talked to them for a few days, until my mother asked me why I wasn't talking. I finally told my mother that I wanted to join the MOP. She was hesitant, but I was determined and told her that whether she accepted it or not I was going to join them; I would even fake her signature on the parent's permission slip, if I had to. She finally accepted it.

On January 2004, I went to the MOP monastery and stayed there for two days. I was really touched by their life and work with the residents. I fell in love with that style of life. Finally, two months before graduation of high school, I told my parents that I wanted to become a missionary. My parents were reluctant because they didn't want me to go very far and were not sure that I had a firm commitment. They suggested instead becoming a diocesan priest, so I would stay nearby, or go to college. I told my father that I didn't want to go to college because I would not be happy and might even lose my vocation. I felt I had a call and I didn't want to put it off. I also felt that this was the fulfillment of my mother's promise for me to serve the Lord.

How was your life as a MOP?

I joined the MOP in 2004, first in Naga for my aspirancy, and then I was sent to Jamaica for my novitiate. I realized that the life of the brothers was hard, but I never complained. It was the simplicity of their life that attracted me despite all the challenges. During my early formation, I found something beautiful in the life of the MOP that cannot be expressed in words. I loved the community life. I loved the residents and the life of prayer. My experience in my family helped me to live life with the MOP. My father had taught me about sacrifice, selling charcoal, rising up early in the morning, and helping my family. This early formation prepared me for a life of sacrifice, poverty, and service to the poor.

However, the life as a MOP was not without trials. In my first year after I joined, I had many challenges and a disappointment that upset me so much that I didn't think I could get over it. So one day, I packed up my suitcase and told my formator that I was leaving. I remember my formator telling me that I had a vocation. He asked me to go to the chapel and remember my first desire to serve the Lord, that, therefore, I should be obedient. He asked me to pray about it before leaving. So I went to the chapel and said, "Lord, what do you want from me?" I felt that God wanted me to stay and obey. So I stayed and since then I never considered leaving again. This incident strengthened me. I felt that God had tested me.

How did you adapt in the community and working with the residents?

In living with the brothers and working with the residents, I felt the love and presence of Christ in a very personal way, in a way that I had never felt before. Now, after ten years, I can say that there are always challenges; but overall, I found the Lord in the simplicity of our life, in our community, and in the residents. Living in community we will always run into new challenges, but since I used to live in a large family, this prepared me to mingle with the other brothers. In the community, the brothers are very different. Some are gentle, some are rough, and others are shy. I had to learn how to communicate with all of them. When they behave in a way that I don't like, I never judge them. I just think this is probably the way they are and how they have been brought up in their own family. When we meet new brothers, we get to know them, and sharing with them is a joy. I am shy, but with God's help, all is workable and all is well. I never miss my own family too much because God has now given me a new and bigger family.

What are your main challenges in your daily life?

After living with the MOP community for eleven years,
I learned that God always challenges me by giving me the
tasks I don't like or I don't think I can do. It is the nature of
the cross and a way that leads me to more deeply encounter
the Lord in my weakness. Our founder says, "Obedience is
a miracle worker." If I only do what is easy for me, I will not
grow. When I am challenged to do something that I don't
want, I receive more graces and I discover more possibilities within me that I thought were beyond my reach.

When I was assigned to administer medications to the
residents, I didn't know I was capable of doing it. First of
all, I did not know anything about nursing or about how to
administer medications; furthermore, I was afraid of blood.
Yet, it was where God put me, it is what God wanted me
to do, so I did not just administer medications to the residents but I also treated their wounds. The first time that
I was called to help our nurse, Brother John Paul, to dress
the wounds of a man that was injured, I almost passed
out. Brother John Paul asked me to sit down because I was
fainting. But it never happened again. I discovered something in me that I knew I could never do by myself, but
only by God's grace. Obedience sets you free; it opens new
possibilities that you did not know existed.

Do you feel the presence of God in your daily tasks?

When I work with the residents, I see Christ in them.
If I am discouraged or need a new boost of energy, I go
to prayer in the chapel. I get my strength from God when

I pray, and beyond all the difficulties and challenges, I encounter the Lord. If I see the Lord in each resident, then I know that whatever I do for him, I do for the Lord.

During my workday, I encounter the Lord in different ways. There was a time when I was cleaning all alone and the work I had to do was quite overwhelming. I thought I would never finish. All of a sudden, a resident came by, calling me and shaking me, "Brother, I can help you! I can also work!" He came back with a shovel, put it right into the dirt and started picking up the garbage alongside me. I realized that God was telling me, "I am going to help you, don't worry, you don't have to do it all by yourself."

Another day, I was administering medications to one of the residents who had been unconscious for several days. I did not know what had happened to him. I kept treating him day after day and whispering in his ear a word of encouragement. After a few days, I saw this man in a wheelchair waving at me. He recognized me and said, "Thank you, brother!" In his unconsciousness, I never knew that he was even noticing me.

On another occasion, a resident that I had been taking care of for some time at the Faith Center who was very sick eventually recovered, and I met him one morning. He yelled, "Brother, thank you, I am fine!" If these residents who seemed to be totally unaware of what was going on and what I was doing for them were grateful for my help, I know that God who sees everything is much more grateful.

Another time I was working at the Lord's Place. A patient with AIDS, sent to us from the hospital because they no longer could do anything for him, had a pressure ulcer—it was so deep that I could see his bone. Before I would get in bed, I used to pray, "Lord, let me see him again tomorrow."

One evening, I was trying to put an IV in him and couldn't find his veins. He told me, "Brother, don't worry, I am okay."

"Let me try one more time," I said.

He told me, "Don't worry, brother. You will try tomorrow."

The next morning I did put in an IV. He was very grateful. After a few days he died. I felt happy caring for somebody who was dying. The Lord showed me that I am not looking after just the residents, but after Him. I thanked the Lord for revealing himself to me through these sick residents that I was tending to.

In which center do you find the greatest challenge?

Bethlehem always challenges me, because it requires taking care of babies and young children. Looking after them is rewarding and hard at the same time. They are young and innocent, and they are suffering deeply. But they always smile at you. It always reminds me that I should be like one of them—trusting, innocent, and always with a smile. The secret of being joyful and staying in love is being in touch with the Lord and never taking your eyes away from him.

Do the residents teach you some lessons?

I learn a lot from the residents. One day, I was in the hospital emergency room, accompanied by one of our mentally retarded residents, Adrian. We had brought to the emergency room another mentally retarded resident who was very sick. This resident kept on repeating, "Lord God," while pointing to his IV that was put in his arm; he wanted to remove it. I drew closer to his bed while holding his hand. The nurses put him in the elevator to take him to the ward. As soon as we got to the elevator, the nurse told me that he was dead. I was in disbelief; he still felt warm. While waiting for him to be taken to the morgue, I asked Adrian to pray with me the Chaplet of Divine Mercy and the Rosary. This event showed me how special are the poor. Despite the mental retardation, this resident kept on uttering the words "Lord God" until the moment he died. I wish I would do the same before I die. Working with the residents can indeed be tiring and demanding, but I know that I am in the place that God wants me to be. I often overflow with joy.

Do you share these experiences with your own family?

Two years ago, when I went home to take my final vows, I shared all these experiences with my parents. While I was there, my father was diagnosed with liver cancer. I showed my father a video of the MOP and the work we do; my father was happy and touched by my work. I told him, "Pa, you are the one who taught me to do this."

My father told me, "The answer is prayer."

With the experience I acquired helping the residents, I was able to take care of my father. I told him, "See how the Lord prepared me to take care of you." My visit prepared him for his death; he died—Christ through my vocation and life as a MOP brother.

At the end of the day, I am full of joy. I told my family, the joy I have comes from the poor I serve, from the crucified Christ in the cross. I would not get this joy from anything else. I found something here that I would never find outside. Our work allows us to become more prayerful and be aware of the presence of the Lord. The joy, the beauty, the depth, the life of the brothers, the brotherhood—it is really the joy of the Lord. he gives us much more than we give to him. Knowing the Lord personally, touching him, this is what we proclaim. This is what I discovered. At the heart of the brothers' vocations is the personal encounter with the Lord. He showers us with his life, his grace, and his joy in abundance.

> *You anoint my head with oil,*
> *my cup overflows.*
> *Surely goodness and mercy shall follow me all*
> *the days of my life;*
> *and I shall dwell in the house of the LORD for*
> *ever.* (Ps 23:5–6)

Chapter Eleven

THE JOYFUL SACRIFICE FOR SALVATION

Brother Paulo Llarena, MOP

But the souls of the righteous are in the hand of
    God,
and no torment will ever touch them. . . .
God tested them and found them worthy of
    himself;
like gold in the furnace, he tried them,
and like a sacrificial burnt offering he accepted
    them.
In the time of their visitation they will shine
    forth,
and will run like sparks through stubble.

Ws 3:1, 5-7

I met Brother Paulo at Bethlehem Center. He shared the story of his vocation journey with me while we were having lunch. He recounts that he came from a very poor family in the Philippines. He never had considered a vocation or had ever thought about joining any religious congregation whatsoever.

When he was fifteen years old, he lost his mother. His heart was so full of grief that during the night, he would find himself inconsolably crying for his mother and worrying if she would be in heaven. He would dream of his mother every night and felt his mother was calling him to do something with his life. One day, when he woke up, he spoke to the Lord and bargained with him: "Lord, I will consecrate my life to you. I will do whatever you want me to do and go wherever you need me to pay the debt of my mother, so you will take her to heaven."

A year and a half later, the MOP visited his parish and invited him to join them. He felt that by joining the MOP he would fulfill the promise he had made to the Lord to give up his life, so his mother could enjoy eternal life with God.

Brother Paulo joined the MOP and his life was transformed. He serves the Lord; he offers his daily sacrifices; so his mother can attain her salvation. He says that the life of the MOP is a life of sacrifice and of giving oneself completely to God, but he says that he gives his life every day without counting the cost and without complaint; he has made a commitment of living a life of sacrifice and of giving himself for the forgiveness of sins, and for the salvation of his mother. He feels at peace and lives in joy and happiness believing that his life has a new meaning: to serve the poor, offering his sacrifices for the salvation of many.

Community life is joyous, Brother Paulo says: "We play, we pray, we share our joy, and sometimes we also experience hardships. But I remind myself that I am serving the Lord. If I am down, I go to God. And if I make a mistake, the love of God is there to forgive my mistakes. It motivates me knowing that the love and mercy of God are always there available. I take all my struggles to the Lord. It makes me stronger; it gives me the fuel that I need to continue my work."

Where do you get your daily strength?

My daily strength relies in keeping my eyes fixed on the Lord and being always grateful to him. Remembering the day my mother died gives me inspiration to continue offering my sacrifices. I am faithful to God; I remember always to thank God for my life and for my blessings. Daily Mass, prayer, and meditations keep me united to God. God is my closest friend, always available to help, to share in my life, at all times. God is always close at hand, always there. We pray four times a day, and in addition, I still have my own prayers before I go to bed, sometimes more intimate and effective than those in the community. We also have retreats throughout the year to charge our spiritual life. The work we do cannot be done without prayer.

Do you sometimes feel discouraged?

Yes, many times. Sometimes it is hard. I take the struggles to God in daily prayer. If I have a problem with a brother, I may also address the problems with the brother in question and always resolve them. God's grace is always available to help us in our struggles.

Where do you like to serve?

Wherever the Lord sends me. Every place is good if it is the will of God. I have no dreams of my own; I leave it to God to guide me through my superiors.

Do you miss your family?

At the beginning, I missed my family very much. Now, I don't miss them so much anymore. It is part of the cross that we carry, renouncing our families. Even if a member is dying, we cannot go there. We only can pray for them.

Chapter Twelve

....

LIFE AS A JOYFUL STRUGGLE

Brother Roche Tulalian, MOP

My son, if you come forward to serve the Lord,
remain in justice and in fear,
and prepare yourself for temptation.
Set your heart right and be steadfast,
incline your ear, and receive words of under-
standing,
and do not be hasty in time of calamity.
Await God's patience, cling to him and do not
depart,
that you may be wise in all your ways.

Sir 2:1-3

"FOR the Missionaries of the Poor, life is a joyful struggle," says Brother Roche. "As MOP, our motto is 'Joyful Service with Christ on the Cross' . . . in Latin 'Servitium Dulce Cum Christo Crucifixo.'"

Tell me about your background and how you came to join the MOP.

I was born and grew up in a family of farmers in the Philippines, a devout Catholic family who brought me up to this stage. My mother prayed the Rosary every night with her five children. After the second decade of the Rosary, one by one we would start falling asleep. A couple of times, I noticed my mother was the only one praying the Rosary while we were all asleep. Noticing it, I began staying awake and praying the whole Rosary with her every night and eventually all my siblings did too. We were young children, but praying together, praying the Rosary in family was an experience that remains engraved in my heart.

When I was young, I had to learn to accept our daily struggles in life—not grudgingly but with a happy and joyful spirit because there were a lot of ups and downs in that journey. My father died when I was four years old, leaving my mom alone to take care of four boys and a girl on the way. I can still recall one night when I heard someone crying. I woke up and looked around, and there I saw my mother kneeling down in front of the altar in our house. I heard her saying, "Lord, how will I manage to raise these children?" Though I was four years old, I could sense that my mother was carrying a very heavy burden of caring for us. Her faith and love for God strengthened her to persevere through the difficult times. Now, I realize that life is full of sorrowful mysteries, the mysteries of light, of joy, and of glory that flow from that divine love that Jesus shared with all of us through his birth, proclamation of the kingdom of God, his passion, death, and resurrection.

To attend Sunday Mass was a struggle for us because we needed to wake up early so we could be at church on time, at 7:30 a.m. We lived in a village in the province of Catanduanes, far from the town where there was a church, and we needed to pass through rice fields and a river to attend Sunday Mass. My mother was always very strict about never missing Mass on Sundays.

I went to a private high school, The Sisters of Mary, founded in Korea by Father Aloysius Schwartz. They had a branch in the Philippines run by nuns. They helped poor children who could not afford to pay for school; they offered tuition and board totally free for four years. It was the best school I could ever have attended. It had excellent academics and faith formation. The sisters taught us how to become saints.

When I was a senior in high school, two MOP, Father Brian Kerr and Brother Augusto Silot Jr., came to our school to recruit vocations. They shared with us their life and work and at the end of their presentation, they gave us a test with some basic questions about our faith. Father Brian told us to pray that the Lord would tell us what He wanted from us while we waited for the results of the exam.

The simplicity of the brothers struck me; they radiated holiness and joy. I was then sixteen years old. Their visit had a deep impact in me. I kept on thinking, "For what will it profit a man, if he gains the whole world and forfeits his life?" (Mt 16:26). This phrase kept on coming to my mind and made me think and reflect on my final destination. I prayed to God to help me discover my vocation and to know his will.

A month later, I got a letter in the mail from the MOP, saying that I had passed the test and that they would welcome me to their "Come and See" program. They also reminded me to get permission from my parents first. I wasn't sure yet if I wanted to attend the program; I didn't want to commit myself to something and then back out. I would take it as a failure and I didn't want to fail. Nevertheless, I did write to my mother asking for her permission to join them in this program. In response to my letter, she told me that if I wanted that life, and if that life would make me happy and fulfilled, then she would totally support me. She said, "You are the one who is going to live it every day, not me. So if you know that God is calling you to be a Missionary of the Poor, I will fully support you with my prayers." Those words had a deep impact in my choice to become what I am now.

Right after graduation in high school, twenty-five classmates traveled with me to the MOP mission in Naga, Philippines to participate in the "Come and See" program. We arrived at their monastery at 4:00 a.m.; the brothers waited for our arrival and prepared for us a very sumptuous meal, welcoming us warmly. We had an orientation and a tour of the apostolate center for the homeless and destitute. The residents were crippled, paralyzed, and with different kinds of disabilities. Meanwhile, the brothers were bathing, clothing, feeding them, and cleaning the place. I asked myself, "Is this the life that God is calling me to?" In my heart, I heard the voice: "If God calls you, will you accept?" I felt that God was calling me and I felt compelled to answer "yes." So I said, "Yes, I accept it!" I felt joyful and privileged that God would choose me despite my weaknesses. I felt that taking care of these children was a privilege. I was called to be in his service.

After the "Come and See" retreat, our superior, Father
Brian Kerr, told us, "Okay, brothers, so are you going to
stay, or go back home and come back?" I raised my hand
to go home for a visit and come back, but he told me,
"Brother, you cannot go home, you need to stay back." I
guess he thought that if I were to go home, I would not
come back. So, I stayed and lived with the brothers. I found
the community prayer very nourishing and helpful to
become more spiritual and to find holiness in life. Prayer
was the key to remain in the community. Prayer was also
essential for living always in the presence of God. Living in
their community was also very fulfilling and important for
my formation and growth.

Do you find the community life with the MOP easy?

The life of the MOP is not easy. Corrections, obedience,
and sacrifice are daily hardships. But there is a purpose for
all of that, and it consists in the fulfillment of our motto:
"Joyful Service with Jesus on the Cross," which teaches all
of us to carry the cross joyfully. And we respond by embracing all the problems and difficulties of daily life, including
the problems with our own brothers. We cannot run away
from each other. We have to learn how to live with each
other. When I am disappointed, I go to the chapel and pray
about it, and I may go to the superior to discuss it too if necessary. The Lord is key; He knows what the problem is and
how to resolve it. Unresolved matters need to be addressed
with God to help us to deal with problems. The advice from
the superior is important too. Carrying the cross with joy

involves carrying the burden of rejections, insults, and idle words.

After joining the MOP, Brother Roche stayed with them in the Philippines for one year. At the end of the year, he went to visit his family and then went back for another year. Along the way, he did entertain doubts, sometimes asking if he was going to be able to endure the MOP life for the rest of his life. And as he recounts, he battled through all the phases of the MOP preparation, but with God's grace and inspiration and the encouragement of his brothers, he persevered.

Are you grateful to your family for your upbringing?

I told my family, I am happy to be here and God blesses you, too, for letting me go. They were invited to come to visit me during my postulancy. We gave them a tour of our centers and invited them to work with the children. My mother was very happy and taken aback by what we were doing. She was moved and inspired. As she was leaving she told me, "If I only knew there was such a community before, I would have joined." She saw God's love displayed through the life of the brothers.

I went home again to see my family before I was sent to Jamaica in 2002. I have been a MOP now for fifteen years. At first, I missed my family. Dealing with people, brothers, residents, and even visitors was hard to handle in some cases. Yet, I accept everybody as they are.

Do you experience new growth in the Lord as years go by?

Yes, more and more every day. There are always lots of struggles, like my personal weaknesses that hinder me in serving him wholeheartedly. Once again, the Lord is always at hand to help. Daily experiences of my prayer life, dealing with my own brothers and the poor are occasions for growth. Through all these daily encounters with God, I get new meaning and purpose in my vocation.

Do you experience moments of dryness?

Yes, there are times in which I don't want to pray and I struggle in prayer. I wrestle with the Lord. I tell the Lord, "You brought me here, but now are you going to leave me in the darkness? Why do I feel this way?" The Lord is faithful; he is always there ready to pick me up. Even when I want to do some good and it is hard to do, I go to prayer for strength. I get up, brush myself off, and start again. The Lord tells me that if I want to follow him, I need to pick up my cross every day, not just once in a while, and follow him. As the years passed, I feel that the Lord has tested my vocation in many ways and occasions to see how deep was my love for him and how far I would go for him. Responses to these questions brought clarity in my life. I have learned to surrender myself up to him completely, even in the periods of darkness. The power of God comes to me through prayer. My community has also helped me to grow in grace and in appreciation for the life that God has given me. The humility to seek help is also a very important tool in fighting through the dark periods.

Can you describe some special moments of consolation or reassurance that the Lord is present in your life?

I have certainly had some special moments where I see the Lord present during my work and prayer. In one occasion, I went down to help the Brothers in the center. Somebody called me to pick up a man in the hospital that had nowhere to go. I said, "Let me check with the brothers to see if we have space." I was told that there was no room available.

The following day, the man made it all the way to our center and called me saying, "I am here in your center." The brothers went to check him out and brought him in. I talked to him and he told me that he had no family and no place to go. I told him that we had no place at our centers either. I asked him to come back in one week. But I noticed that he was weary, dirty, and his clothes were raggedy. I told him to wait and I came back with food and clothes. He asked me to change the wheel in his wheelchair because it was broken. I didn't know how to fix it, so I called the brothers for help. A brother fixed it, but he was still there waiting for me. I noticed that he was smelly and filthy, so I asked to bathe him before we would discharge him. He told me that for six months, he had never bathed. We spent three hours bathing, dressing, treating his wounds, and feeding him. He said, "Brothers, thank you for what you did to me." I felt it was Christ telling me, "As you did it to the least of these my brethren, you did it to me" (Mt 25:40). These words were being fulfilled in my presence. I still didn't know what to do with him. Was I going to send him back? Where would he go? I couldn't release him, so I asked the brother to let him rest there in a bed. He immediately fell in a deep sleep and we let him stay. The following day I went to visit him. He was so happy! "Brother, I feel at home here!" I could not throw the Lord out of our home! His name is Henry and he still lives with us. By simply feeding the residents and seeing their gratefulness, you get back a very rewarding joy. The presence of brothers and volunteers makes the residents very happy and we share in that happiness.

Did you experience hard and difficult times as a MOP?

Certainly. In particular, when an assassin killed two of our brothers, Brother Suresh and Brother Marco. It was hard, but that tragedy brought blessings to our community and especially to each one of us. This was a reassurance that the Lord blesses our community that is founded in his very own life, in a way of living it out in a radical way of poverty and vulnerability. This event, rather than weakening me, gave me the strength and courage to persevere in giving my entire life to the service of God, my community, and the poor we served daily.

Which vow is the hardest for you?

Obedience, which I belief affects the other vows. As St.
Ignatius of Loyola says, "As long as obedience is flourishing, all the other virtues will be seen to flourish and to bear
fruit." Obedience is against our rebellious nature, especially
when a young brother corrects you. My tendency is to dis-
miss him; you do not want younger people to correct you.
I feel like I know better than them. But then, as a professed
brother, I know how to exercise humility; we are trained
how to accept commands and corrections. Our superior is,
in some cases, a younger and more inexperienced brother.
We are trained in handling that. It becomes easier as we
grow older. Obedience helps us in our spiritual growth,
too. Sometimes the brothers are sharp and command you
in a hurtful way. But you realize that it is an opportunity for
self-denial and self-control. Other times, I might get irri-
tated. If I do, I apologize to the brother. Situations come
and go. The best thing to do is to let go.

**Do you ever have temptations to go back to the world
and be free?**

It does come and go, especially during prayer when your
mind is relaxed. I personally feel that it is useless to think
about it. And I recognize it as coming from a bad spirit,
a temptation—I reject it. In those instances, I go back to
my vows and remember the promises I made, to give my
life to God, and this is what I am called to do. I pray for
perseverance, strength, and faithfulness to my vows and
vocation. The evil attacks us in our weakness and even in

our strengths. Sometimes your weakness becomes your strength, and your strength your weakness. It is tricky and an everyday battle. We need to be faithful until the day that we will hear: "Come, O blessed of my Father, inherit the kingdom prepared for you from the foundation of the world; for I was hungry and you gave me food, I was thirsty and you gave me drink, I was a stranger and you welcomed me, I was naked and you clothed me, I was sick and you visited me, I was in prison and you came to me. . . . Truly, I say to you, as you did it to one of the least of my brethren, you did it to me" (Mt 25:34-40).

Do you miss your family?

Yes, sometimes. I remember one day when my mother wrote to me and told me, "I was sick for a month, and the only thing I did was to pray and think of you. You were serving others and I was alone, yet I look at Jesus on the cross and he was alone too. I also realized that I am helping you with my suffering, which I have been offering for you." It is a sacrifice for us, too, to see that we cannot help our relatives when they need us. Yet, my mother was sick, offering her sacrifices for me. This is the mystery and beauty of the communion of the saints. We are praying and sacrificing for each other. My mother is also helping me in my way to sanctity.

Who shall separate us from the love of Christ?
Shall tribulation, or distress, or persecution, or
famine, or nakedness, or peril, or sword? . . . For
I am sure that neither death, nor life, nor angels,

*nor principalities, nor things present, nor things
to come, nor powers, nor height, nor depth, nor
anything else in all creation, will be able to separate us from the love of God in Christ Jesus our
Lord.* (Rom 8:35, 38-39)

Chapter Thirteen

TO CHRIST THROUGH PRAYER

Brother (Spo) Simon Peter Omolo, MOP

For whoever does the will of my Father in heaven is my brother, and sister, and mother.

Mt 12:50

"I was born in Kenya. I am one of five siblings. My parents are practicing Catholics and married in the Church. They baptized all of us in the Catholic Church when we were infants. They taught us to love the Lord and love each other. Both my parents are wonderful. My grandfather was Anglican, and my grandmother was Catholic. She brought up all her children as Catholic. This was remarkable for a woman of that time. To go to Mass on Sunday was not easy; we had to walk through rough areas and forests for a long distance.

"My grandmother wished that one of her grandchildren would serve the Lord in a religious order. She asked all of us boys to be altar boys. I was very inspired by the missionaries who would come by and preach to us. When I was twenty-four, my grandmother died and her prayer to have a grandson serving the Lord came true.

129

"When I was in grade four, I became seriously ill. The doctors could not diagnose my ailment. Through this illness, God was calling me to seek him. One of my father's friends advised me to seek healing in a prayer group led by a charismatic priest considered to be a healer. I attended a healing service, but while many of the participants were healed through the priest's invocation of the name of Jesus and the laying on of his hands, I was not. At the end of the healing service, the priest told me, 'Do not be afraid; if you don't get healed now, it will happen later, in God's own time.' I can say that from this healing service, the Lord made me more patient. I no longer felt fearful or worried; I was given the grace of letting go and trusting in God.

"After I finished school, I went to work as a security guard in a neighborhood school. I told the priest running that school that I wanted to become a priest. He realized that the Lord was calling me to work as a missionary in his vineyard and he put me in contact with the MOP. I applied to their order, and they invited me to go to the 'Come and See' program in Kenya. I joined a group of forty other candidates attending this program; at the end only twelve remained. As the Lord said, 'Many are called, but few are chosen' (Mt 22:14). I felt happy and privileged to be counted among the chosen ones."

Was it easy to adapt to the MOP life?

The life of the MOP is not easy. To keep the vows is not easy; obedience is the hardest and highest vow and somehow it embodies all the other vows. St. Ignatius of Loyola said, "As long as obedience is flourishing, all the other virtues will be seen to flourish and to bear fruit." If you break any other vow, you disobey. Chastity is a very delicate vow too. Temptations come and go. Lust makes you blind, but you need to be connected to God to see your imperfections; you need to pray to detect and avoid them. If we do not obey, it is obvious to yourself and others, but if we are not chaste—especially when it is in our thoughts, in our mind—it is not so obvious to others. Our mind can be tested with lustful thoughts, but with the grace of God, all is possible to overcome. St. Augustine obtained the grace of chastity through prayer and God's grace. Temptations of the flesh are very common. Prayer is essential for combating temptations.

Since I joined the MOP, I consider all the brothers and the residents as my family. I love these little children at Bethlehem; they are my family too and I am very honored serving them. I feel that when I am caring for these children, I am tending to the wounds of Jesus and I experience His presence in them. All God's creation is good; we are all precious in God's eyes, regardless of our physical or mental handicaps. It encourages me to ponder the words of Jesus: "Whatever you do for one of these little ones, you did it for me" (see Mt 25:40) and "Whosoever takes care of the poor will not be abandoned" (see Prv 28:27). God keeps on reminding me of the sanctity of my work. He is present in my work as he is when I am in prayer.

What propels you in your work?

I consider prayer as the first and foremost part of my life. Union with God through prayer strengthens us for the battle. If we don't pray, Satan attacks. The devil is like a roaring lion looking for someone to devour (see 1 Pt. 5:8). We cannot withstand the temptations of the devil with our human strength. We need God's grace and help, and we get it in the measure that we need it and above. Prayer is fundamental to resist the temptations of the evil one; whether you are a MOP, single, or a married person you need prayer to withstand temptation. From prayer comes the grace to solve any and all problems.

Are you happy in your new life?

I am happy and joyful since I joined the MOP. When people see me, I want them to see Christ alive in me. I want them to see that there is hope in the world. I am an instrument of God, and I do my work with joy. God loves a joyful giver and wants us to always be joyful givers. I do my work with the strength that comes from God. We are nothing by ourselves. Everything that is good comes from God. I do not boast about anything because all my goodness comes from God. Whatever I have I give back; I receive freely and give back freely. When I die, I will say I wish I could have done more. My family is proud of me. When I go home, everybody comes to see me; they feel I am a blessing to them and to their town. They feel blessed by me being a MOP.

Rejoice in the Lord always; again I will say, Rejoice. Let all men know your forbearance. The Lord is at hand. Have no anxiety about anything, but in everything by prayer and supplication with thanksgiving let your requests be made known to God. And the peace of God, which passes all understanding, will keep your hearts and your minds in Christ Jesus. (Phil 4:4-7)

Chapter Fourteen

....

LITTLE HEAVEN ON EARTH

Brother Prasant, MOP

*Truly, I say to you, there is no one who has
left house or brothers or sisters or mother or
father or children or lands, for my sake and for
the gospel, who will not receive a hundredfold
now in this time, houses and brothers and sisters
and mothers and children and lands, with perse-
cutions, and in the age to come eternal life.*

Mk 10:29–30

BROTHER Prasant comes from northern India. He is
the youngest and the only male of four siblings. He felt
a call to the religious life since he was in elementary school.
In 2004, he attended a vocation camp and contacted four
religious orders expressing his desire to join them. No one
wrote him back. He continued his studies until 2006 when
a friend told him about the MOP. He contacted them and
his life changed forever.

"I shared with my mother my vocation and interest to
join a religious order. She was not interested and tried to
dissuade me because I was the only male in the family. I
also began to doubt my vocation and decided that I should
go back to study. When I was riding a bus to go to college,

135

I met a MOP and introduced myself. The brother told me about his life and the MOP work; I told him that I was interested in joining them, and he gave me the contact information of their mission in southern India. I debated whether to serve the Lord or heed the advice of my mother, staying home, something that my mother wanted for her only son. I decided to join and stay with the MOP and serve the Lord. I went to the MOP monastery in southern India and stayed with them from 2007 to 2009. From India, I was sent to Jamaica to continue my formation in the novitiate and to work and serve the poorest of the poor in their apostolate centers."

How has your life been in the MOP community so far?

My life as a MOP is very happy and filled with joy. I have no regrets. For me, the community is a little heaven on earth. All the sacrifices I make are nothing compared to what I gain. All my sacrifices help me to obtain eternal life.

We have struggles living in our community, but the prayer, daily Masses, meditations, and the congregation keeps us focused on our vocation and our mission. With full confidence, I can say that from prayer, I get my strength and confidence to withstand all the challenges of the day. Prayer helps me to carry my cross. I know that I am following the way of the cross, I am laying down my life for God every day, serving and loving him in the needy people.

How do you like working at Bethlehem Center?

When I was assigned to Bethlehem Center, I asked the Lord to give me the strength and grace to love the children. I really saw the struggle and pain of Jesus on the cross in them. Like Jesus, they cannot leave the cross; the children are nailed to their cribs without the possibility of getting up and moving. In them, I hear the cry of Jesus on the cross, "My God, my God, why have you forsaken me?" (Mt 27:46). God gave me the privilege to serve him and see him suffering and dying on the cross each day in each child here.

Do you find challenges in the life of a MOP?

There are challenges and hardships in the life of the MOP, but with God's grace, everything is possible to overcome. One of the hardest challenges in the life of a MOP is being faithful to our vow of obedience. With my free will, I would like to make choices, yet when I accepted this life, I had to let go of my will and lay down my life. I have to obey others, even when sometimes I would have chosen not to obey. I thank and bless the Lord who has been so good to me. I had no moment of my life that I did not wish to be here. Every morning when I rise, I thank the Lord for blessing me for bringing me here, and I never have a regret.

How would you like people to remember you?

I am a religious brother; I would like to radiate Christ to others with my life. I would like it if, through my life and

love for the residents, the people would see Christ in me. I
want to be a reflection of Christ.

> *Let your light so shine before men, that they*
> *may see your good works and give glory to your*
> *Father who is in heaven.* (Mt 5:16)

CONCLUSION

WHEN I went to visit the Missionaries of the Poor in Jamaica, I had no expectations. I did not know if I was going to have the opportunity to meet and talk to the brothers, or the extent to which I was ready or would be able to work with the residents, or even if I were only to attend a retreat guided by the founder, whom I felt was a very holy and charismatic man who radiated God's presence and through whom God could speak to me. It turned out to be all of the above.

I was particularly struck by the happiness and joy which these holy brothers radiated in their monastery as well in the apostolate centers. The chants, Rosary, liturgy, and even the simple meals shared with the brothers left me and the other volunteers with the impression that we were stepping on holy ground; these men exuded the love and the presence of the divine.

My curiosity as to the manner in which the divine power was affecting their lives and so powerfully radiating it outward to others propelled me to ask them some questions about their journey and experiences. I felt their pathway to sanctity had led them to rapidly advance towards the center of the seven mansions (as described by St. Teresa of Avila in her book *The Interior Castle*), where God abides, in a remarkably short time.

That said, many of the brothers are very young and experience temptations, doubts, and the siren call of the world—to say nothing of the physical trials and illnesses such work entails—but they also receive extraordinary graces from God. They are reassured—some through astonishing manifestations of Divine Providence and mystical visions—that they really serve, see, touch, and clean the face of God present in the most needy people.

During my visits, the brothers shared stories of their work with me. I felt that that these stories should not remain untold. I never intended to become the instrument to bring these amazing accounts to the readers of this book. In fact, I suggested to one of the brothers that he write and publish his story. My suggestion was dismissed with a glimpse of humility and shyness. So, I, too, dropped the idea and it was not until some time later that the Holy Spirit would prompt me to write *My Brother's Keeper*, in which the brothers themselves would tell us how they came to trod this radical path of Christian life.

You, readers of these stories, without leaving the comfort of your home, have stepped on holy ground. Through reading of these young men and their love for God and neighbor, you have been invited to feel the very presence of God. One of the visitors to the MOP, who read the stories collected in this book, shared with me her impression: "The brothers' stories touched my heart and made me want to kneel down to worship our Savior. Their stories led me to examine and meditate upon what I am doing with my life, my witness, the path I am walking, and where I am going. Their stories strengthened me to strive toward holiness."

This collection of the brothers' biographies was written so that young and old people alike may come to fully understand the voice of Pope St. John Paul II who, when addressing the multitude gathered for Youth Day, said, "Do not be afraid to say yes to Jesus Christ. He will take nothing from you; He will give you everything."

These words of the Holy Father, who touched so many young peoples' lives, are fulfilled in those of the brothers. They have lost nothing; they have gained everything. The brothers shared their stories not as an act of pride for saying yes to God, nor because they want to see their biographies written (most of them felt shy and too insignificant to even think that someone would want to write about them), but because they want the world to know how the power of God, working in and through our nothingness, regardless of our state in life, can lead us to sanctity. Their stories are written for the greater glory of God.

Appendix

....

PONTIFICAL RECOGNITION MASS OF THANKSGIVING

(A Recollection by the Author)

> *Brothers and sisters, it is a new time in our*
> *Church, a new age, a new springtime. . . . The*
> *faith of the poor and the faith that carries us to*
> *the poor are most beautiful. Happiness lies in*
> *serving the poor and serving one another.*
>
> From the homily by Father Ho Lung during
> the Pontifical Mass of Thanksgiving

O N April 26, 2015, one of the most significant milestones in the life of the MOP took place in Jamaica—the Pontifical recognition of their order by Pope Francis. I felt honored to be invited to attend this celebration. Initially, I had thought that the long trip and cost involved to attend the Mass was too burdensome. God, however, removed all obstacles in unexpected ways, so I went back to Jamaica a week in advance to attend the Mass and work in the centers. God was calling me back.

The week before the celebration went by quickly. Working again in Bethlehem and Jacob's Well and attending retreats and celebrations was truly glorious. The visitors

143

were invited to go to the Corpus Christi Center to participate in two hours of adoration of the Blessed Sacrament
and to listen to meditations guided by Father Richard Ho
Lung. The presence of God there was real, and it filled that
place. We received grace upon grace throughout the week,
including being present at the profession of vows of twenty
new brothers in a Mass officiated by the Archbishop of the
Caribbean. How special it was to see twenty courageous,
selfless, and brave young men offering their lives to God
and vowing to live in poverty serving the poor. Being in the
patio of Christ the Redeemer and feeling so much joy was
a reminder of Psalm 23:5: "You anoint my head with oil,
/ my cup overflows." Truly, through all these events, God
infused so much love into our souls that it was overflow-
ing. I felt as if the entire experience was like a foretaste of
heaven.

During the week, all the visitors were invited to gather at
the Holy Innocents Center, where the MOP Sisters reside,
for the blessing of new solar panels donated by the German
government. The sisters diligently had prepared a welcoming tent to protect the distinguished guests from the sun
and arranged rows of chairs in front of the tent, under and
around the trees in the patio so all invited could comfort-
ably participate in the event. Father Ho Lung delivered a
welcoming greeting and thanked the German ambassador
and his delegation for the generous donation of the solar
panels and their significance in easing the electrical burdens of the center. We all participated in the tour as the
engineers explained how those "solar cells" were able to
store and convert the solar energy into electricity during

the long sunny hours of the day in Jamaica. This reminded me of the MOP as "spiritual cells" that harness together the energies of love to feed and care for thousands of hungry and needy people.

Finally, the climax of that special week took place on Sunday, April 26, 2015, when—with a group of volunteers from Christ the Redeemer led by Father Max—we walked to the Holy Trinity Cathedral to celebrate their Pontifical Recognition Mass of Thanksgiving.

The awesome splendor of Kingston Holy Trinity Cathedral on North Street in Kingston welcomed us. The Cathedral was built in 1911 in the Byzantine Revival style, replacing the Holy Trinity Church built in 1811, which was destroyed in the 1907 earthquake. Its eighty-five foot high copper-covered dome stood like a beacon welcoming the guests inside. As we entered, I was stunned by the magnificent three thousand square feet of murals and frescoes in its ceiling. No wonder it is considered one of the most beautiful churches in both Jamaica and the wider Caribbean. I learned that the Jesuit lay brother Francis Schroen created the artwork and that the new murals were painted over in the 1970s because, unfortunately, the old ones had deteriorated. Many of the glass windows had been destroyed by the hurricane in 1951 and the broken glass had been replaced with stained glass panels featuring St. Josephine Bakhita, St. Martin de Porres, Pierre Toussaint, and others. This cathedral that had once welcomed Pope St. John Paul II was now welcoming the Missionaries of the Poor for their summit celebration as an Institute of Pontifical Right.

Over two hundred MOP Brothers, most of the MOP Sisters, the founder Father Richard Ho Lung, and first founding members Father Brian Kerr and Father Hayden Augustine, Kelvin Cardinal Felix from the Caribbean, bishops, archbishops, including Archbishop Charles Dufour from Jamaica, nuncio of the Holy See Archbishop Nicola Girasoli, clergy, residents from all the different centers, friends, benefactors, and well-wishers from all over the world packed the sacred space to capacity.

Music sung by the brothers and by the choir of "Father Ho Lung and Friends" was bringing the dome and walls of the Cathedral down! It was as if all the choirs of angels in heaven were bursting into song in celebration with us. Truly, the glory of God filled the temple! The Mass and whole ceremony lasted four hours in a packed church without air conditioning on an unbearably hot day. We all seemed to forget the heat and sweat as we participated in the liturgy, prayers, and songs. We were all joined in celebrating that memorable event that meant so much to the MOP institute and to the universal Church. "Brothers and sisters, it is a new time in our Church, a new age, a new springtime. . . . The faith of the poor and the faith that carries us to the poor are most beautiful. Happiness lies in serving the poor and serving one another," Father Richard Ho Lung expressed in his homily. What a privilege I felt being part of that magnificent celebration! I understood what it means to be a temple built with living stones!

ABOUT THE AUTHOR AND EDITOR

CARMEN Vigo was born and raised in Spain. She now lives in California. She has an undergraduate degree in nuclear physics from the University of Madrid, Spain, and a Ph.D. in Biochemistry from the University of London, Royal College of Surgeons of England. She is the mother of three children and the author of numerous scientific papers and patents. She has made several trips to Jamaica since 2014 to attend a retreat with Father Richard Ho Lung and volunteer with the Missionaries of the Poor.

Monica Yoshida worked closely with her mother, Carmen Vigo, editing this book. She graduated from the University of San Diego with a B.A. in English and Psychology. Upon graduation, she pursued a professional classical ballet career, dancing in Spain and the United States. She also followed her interest in healthcare, working as a CNA/ Counselor at Lucille Packard Children's Hospital and as a Nurse Tech at Mary Free Bed Rehabilitation Hospital. She now resides in San Diego with her husband and newborn daughter.

ABOUT THE AUTHOR
AND EDITOR